*f*P

# The iConnected Parent

Staying Close to Your Kids in College (and Beyond)
While Letting Them Grow Up

Barbara K. Hofer, Ph.D.,
and Abigail Sullivan Moore

Free Press

New York   London   Toronto   Sydney

FREE PRESS

A Division of Simon & Schuster, Inc.
1230 Avenue of the Americas
New York, NY 10020

First Free Press hardcover edition August 2010

FREE PRESS and colophon are trademarks of Simon & Schuster, Inc.

For information about special discounts for bulk purchases, please contact Simon & Schuster Special Sales at 1-866-506-1949 or business@simonandschuster.com.

The Simon & Schuster Speakers Bureau can bring authors to your live event. For more information or to book an event contact the Simon & Schuster Speakers Bureau at 1-866-248-3049 or visit our website at www.simonspeakers.com.

Designed by Carla Jayne Jones

Manufactured in the United States of America

10   9   8   7   6   5   4   3   2   1

Library of Congress Cataloging-in-Publication Data

Hofer, Barbara K.

The iConnected parent: staying close to your kids in college (and beyond) while letting them grow up / Barbara K. Hofer and Abigail Sullivan Moore.—1st ed.
p. cm.
1. Parenting. 2. Parent and teenager. 3. College students—conduct of life. 4. College students—Social networks. I. Moore, Abigail Sullivan. II. Title.
HQ755.8.H59 2010
646.7'80842—dc22

2010002637

ISBN 978-1-4391-4829-7
ISBN 978-1-4391-5418-2 (ebook)

# Note to Readers - - - - - - - - - - - - - - - - - - - - - - - - - - - - - - -

Names of students and other young adults portrayed in this book have been changed, with the exception of the students who conducted research with Barbara Hofer. In all instances, names of parents identified solely by a first name have been changed.

To our children, Selene and Zach, Jack and Carlos, and to the memory of our parents

# Contents

Contents

# The
# iConnected
# Parent

# iConnected Parenting 101

Michelle is a college sophomore who calls her parents three times a day. "It's very comforting. Once in the evening, once during the day, and once before bed—I will talk to them about whatever," she says, while eating lunch with her roommate at a private university in Connecticut. With her hip navy hoodie and attitude to match, Michelle blends right into this cafeteria crowd. She does not blush or whisper as she reveals how close she is to her parents; her roommate doesn't even arch a perfectly waxed eyebrow, because she too is in daily contact with her family. They both glance at their cell phones, sitting at the ready, nestled next to their plates of fries and chicken tenders. "I text, like, all the time to everyone—my friends, my parents. And they text back," says the roommate, who is also unabashed about her close connection to home. What are all the texts about? "The little things, grades, life. If something happens, I'll send a text so I don't have to get involved in a detailed conversation," she says.

Typically she saves these talks with mom or dad for her walks between classes. She is scarcely alone in doing so. Visit any campus at the change of classes and watch the students stream out of buildings to cross green-covered quads or concrete plazas. As if on cue they whip out their cell phones. At the University of Minnesota, Buck often passes his cell phone to his friends, weather permitting. Who is on the phone? His parents, although usually it's his mom, and his buddies want to talk to her too. "I actually love talking to mom and dad on the way to class," says Buck, a junior. "It's kind of a habit now—unless it's something really private. My friends really enjoy my parents and will jump on the phone and talk to them." In high school Buck's mother used to put an encouraging note in his football helmet before each game, a practice so appealing that his teammates asked her for notes too (which she did, even though she worked part-time and had three other kids besides Buck). Now she's updating her tradition, offering inspiration via cell. For her part, she is delighted to do so. She also appreciates her more private talks with Buck: "I find the sweetest conversations are when they're walking to class. You have their undivided attention. Their roommates aren't in the background making noise with the Wii or PlayStation. If they're not around anyone else and if there is something bothering them, there is nothing kept back."

In conversations around the country students are telling parents about their latest breakup, what they are having for lunch, and to *please* edit the term paper they are emailing home and that's due tomorrow. With an affectionate good-bye they click off, ending the connection—though not for long.

This is a world away from the experience of college students and parents even just several years back. We use the term *iConnected Parenting* to refer to a culture of parents deeply involved in their children's lives, even as they approach adulthood, that uses the technology of instant communication to enhance their connection. Perhaps nowhere is this trend more evident than on campus, where parents and kids once separated. We believe that it has substantially changed parent-child relationships, during the college years especially, and that there are both benefits and drawbacks to this.

Not so long ago students left for college and began to make the critical journey from adolescence to adulthood pretty much on their own. They coped with incompatible roommates and demanding professors. They figured out how to do laundry, register for classes, and manage their studies, even if it meant pulling an all-nighter on a term paper they had procrastinated on. And they endured the ups and downs of the campus social scene, sharing first dates and flings with roommates and friends. Along the way they learned how to rely on themselves, discovering when and how to seek help. This was all part of growing up, learning to make decisions without always talking to their parents. By the time the weekly check-in call with the home front rolled around, problems had often been solved and intense feelings over a bad grade, a coach's benching, or a one-night stand had faded.

That was just fine for most families. Parents who had attended college remembered relishing their own newfound independence and believed their kids wanted the same. College was a coming-of-age event, a milestone marking a departure from home and family on the ascent to adulthood. Even parents heavily involved in their kids' lives played by these rules. It wasn't so hard to do. Unless the student attended college close to home, there was no practical way for mom or dad to stay closely engaged.

A child's departure for college was also a milestone for mom and dad. It closed the chapter on one part of their family life and opened another, as they began to treat their college-age children as more adult than adolescent. They too moved on with their lives, freed from their daily child rearing by one less child at home.

## Parenting in an Age of Instant Communication

Today it's a totally different story, and our communications technology and child-centered culture are driving it. Cell phones and the Internet have changed how parents and students communicate during the college years and beyond. Involved parents aren't sure if all this instant access is healthy, but they enjoy the closeness they have with their kids and are proud of it. And they have been so involved with their kids before college that it's hard to stop now, with computers and cell phones forming a continuous cord from home to campus.

We call these caring moms and dads *iConnected Parents*. They represent a new era in parenting: a potent new mix of devoted parent, guide, and friend, fluent in speed-dial, Facebook, and the flick of a mouse.

For the past several years popular media have been reporting widely on signs of this shift: colleges that stage "letting go" seminars for parents of freshmen; families buying homes near campus to be close to their kids; overnight summer camps providing daily email service and website photos for campers and parents; and "emerging adults," delaying the transition to true adulthood as they wrestle with finding just the right career, spouse, or apartment. There has been sensational coverage of "helicopter parents": ambitious but mostly well-meaning parents who completely overmanage their children. The chopper crowd represents only a tiny and extreme segment of iConnected parents, however. The real story has yet to be told, which is why we wrote this book. We cover this shift in technology-enhanced parenting through original research and reporting. We show how technology is changing the dynamics of parent and child relationships, the college experience, and the work world.

Many parents want to know exactly how much and how little to communicate with their growing adult children, and just aren't sure what's best. That's another reason we wrote this book: to provide some guidelines for parents and also to show that this new closeness of communication does have its benefits as well as some drawbacks. You'll see examples of beneficial relationships as well as some that may show the difference between helpfulness and overinvolvement.

In these stories you will also see the many different factors to consider when determining the right amount of communication for you and your child. We have learned from parents that it is often hard to know how much is enough. For instance, one mom requires her 20-year-old son, a college student in New Orleans, to check in with her daily, ever since she couldn't reach him for two days while he was busy rushing for a frat. He had told her about all the drinking that was involved, and she suspected the worst. Even though the rush period is now over, her rule is still in place. Besides, she says, she's also worried about the hazards of living in the Big Easy. "He thinks it's abnormal for a twenty-year-old to check in every day," she said. "It's something that I insist on. My friends say, 'That's overkill.' I don't know if it's overkill exactly. Parents aren't given a lot of direction."

Our ability to communicate with each other so easily seems to have happened overnight. But our cell phones and laptops didn't come with instructions on how to parent with them. Many parents want guidance on how to be connected in a healthy way to their college kids (and in the years just before and after college too). In the chapters ahead we provide that advice, drawing on our research, psychological expertise, and real stories of students, parents, college administrators, professors, psychiatrists, and others.

## Our Stories

As a journalist Abigail Sullivan Moore began her spadework on connected parenting several years ago while regularly contributing stories about college and high school trends to the *New York Times*. As she interviewed parents and students, Abby became intrigued with how close they were. Many parents weren't hovering; they were just more engaged with their children than their own parents had been with them, and they reveled in it—at least most of the time. As a mother of two boys, one now starting college, the other in middle school, Abby saw the parallel in her own life.

Abby's interest in how cell phones affect relationships dates back to an early story that she reported for the *Times* on the risks that people would take to get their cell phones to work in dead zones. Perching in heels atop porch railings, climbing ancient fire escapes, people would do nearly anything to stay connected, and as she learned later that went double for parents and children. The instant access afforded by cell phones and computers was amplifying the connection between parents and kids, although not always for the best. Abby got an inkling of this shortly after getting her own clunky cell phone in the mid-1990s. She interrupted an important interview to take what she thought was an emergency call from the babysitter. As it turned out, it was from her older son, Jack, then 6 years old. "Where are the Doritos?" he asked.

Dr. Barbara Hofer, a researcher and psychology professor at Middlebury College, trained in developmental, educational, and cultural psychology, had begun a quest of her own. Watching the students walk out of her Adolescent Development class and open their cell phones to call home, she wondered how this cultural shift was affecting their development and their growth as learners. This complex question was built on research she had pursued several years earlier while teaching a Learning to Learn course to first-year students. Some of those students seemed unprepared for college because their parents had been overly involved in monitoring their work in high school.

She asked a few students to help her get a research project going that would explore how the frequency of communication with parents, made possible by cell phones, was related to becoming emotionally, behaviorally, and academically independent. The results of that study, reported in the next chapter, got picked up in the popular media and led to further research at Middlebury, a top liberal arts college in Vermont, and the University of Michigan, a large public research university.

The parent of two recent college grads, Barbara was also aware that much had changed in communication practices between college students and their parents in a very short time. The weekly calls her family and others had savored now appeared to have morphed into daily calls among the new crowd of college students, many of whom appeared to be having a harder time living independently.

We authors were on parallel tracks. We met during an interview as Abby pursued a story on this new generation of superconnected parents. We decided to tell the story together in a book. Here we share the results of our reporting and research, offering what we think are useful insights into these cultural changes.

## Cultural Forces Driving iConnected Parenting

The roots of iConnected parenting are embedded in the profound cultural changes in the United States over the past decade. The continually evolving communications technology allows parents and children to stay in constant, instant touch. A lot of families like it that way. Many parents are anxious about the world today, believing it's more dangerous than the one they grew up in, and they see cell phones as a safety net for their kids. In fact parents and students often time their calls for the students' late-night walk from the library to the dorm. It's as if somehow mom or dad, miles away, is still able to protect them.

Today's parents also are passionate about parenting and about being parents. They have had fewer kids and often delayed having them. More parents than ever are working outside the home, away from their kids, and many feel a deep desire to make every second with their kids count. They want to be involved in their children's lives at a level unimaginable to their own parents. Since their own childhood much has changed. The number of kids' activities in and out of school has increased exponentially, and they provide a boatload of opportunities for parents to become and stay involved. These activities create busy schedules, with lots of carpooling and last-minute adjustments. ("Kim's sick today. Can you drive the girls to soccer practice?") With more parents working, business commitments and office hours now figure into the frenetic mix. Calls, texts, and emails have become vital tools for families to manage the endless round of pickups and dropoffs.

Meanwhile the increasing competition for college admissions has created more pressure on kids' performance in school and in the community. That, in turn, has pushed parents to get even more engaged. Again the cell phone and computer have proved indispensable to parents, many of whom worry about their kids' academic performance and want an immediate link to teachers and school administrators.

Given the powerful forces at work here, iConnected parenting now seems an inevitable phenomenon.

## The iConnected Kids

Parents are not alone in their appreciation of and dependence on this link across the ether. Many students expect and even embrace their parents' participation in their campus lives. In the era of iConnected parenting, parents are no longer just one big embarrassment. In fact many of the students we interviewed for this book describe their parents as a "best friend," a description that was unheard of (and perhaps considered pathological) only a decade ago. Again and again students openly and happily expressed affection for their parents. When Frankie Minor, director of residential life at the University of Missouri, strolls across campus, he can't help but overhear bits and pieces of students' cell conversations. He can always tell when they're talking to their parents: "The phrase I hear that clues you in is 'I love you.'"

What a change technology and ten years have wrought! Moms and dads are parenting their kids with the latest technology, and most kids seem to accept it. Those who once may have thought their parenting days were over now find themselves supervising their college-age children, albeit electronically and from afar. And the children? Many seem stuck somewhere between adolescence and adulthood, calling mom and dad all the while. That is, after all, the big downside to this trend.

## The Long and Winding Road to Adulthood

The road to adulthood just keeps getting longer and longer. The years from the late teens to the early 20s have always been a crucial but brief phase before becoming a grown-up; now this too is changing. The new in-between generation is spending more time in this phase, which psychologist Jeffrey Arnett calls "emerging adulthood." In essence they are postponing traditional adulthood. They are taking longer to complete college; it's now closer to five years than four. After college they are choosing more often to live with their parents. They are putting off marriage as well as having children. (The median age of first marriage has risen to 26 for women and 28 for men, up from 20 and 23, respectively, in 1960.) They are taking longer to support themselves. And psychologically they are still trying to figure out who they are and how to navigate the world with a measure of independence.

No doubt some of these changes have been exacerbated by the faltering economy of the first decade of the twenty-first century, but they were evident long before the recession. The proof is everywhere: parents perpetually footing the bill for their aging children's rent, car insurance, clothing, and cell phones while the children search for the perfect career; young people who can't accept a job or negotiate a salary without consulting mom and dad; college grads who move back home and into their high school persona, sleeping late, surrounded by heaps of dirty laundry and a trash can overflowing with fast-food wrappers and other teen-era detritus. Even Hollywood has taken note, producing send-ups such as *Failure to Launch,* with Matthew McConaughey as a 30-something still living at home with his exasperated parents, and *Step Brothers,* with funnymen Will Ferrell and John C. Riley as aging but immature stepchildren learning to live under the same roof. Viewed as a whole, these cultural bits and pieces show a profound change in how our children are growing up, and iConnected parenting is playing a large part in it.

## iConnected Parenting and the College Experience

Without a doubt these close connections are remapping the college experience. The immediacy of cell phones and laptops now brings mom and dad onto campus and right into the classroom. Boring lectures, "mean girl" roommates, difficult tests—parents hear about them instantly.

What a difference from our own experiences. When Abby was a freshman at the University of Pennsylvania and ran into some roommate problems of her own, she solved the problem as best she could, without calling her parents back in Fall River, Massachusetts. She camped out all night to get one of the few remaining rooms (a single on the quad) assigned on a first-come, first-served basis. Her parents learned of the change only weeks later, when she gave them her new mailing address. Though this may not have been the best way to handle her roommate problem, Abby at 17 fixed the situation herself.

Barbara remembers her parents' support on key decisions during the college years. They provided a sounding board, but let her make the choices, and there was no need to consult with them about small issues. When bored with her sophomore year at the University of South Florida, she let her parents know she was considering dropping out and applying to social service programs, taking a paid internship in Washington, or transferring. They listened deeply, asked good questions, but didn't advise. She soon left for Washington, a life-changing experience that fueled her motivation for learning and led her back to college.

Today, of course, things are very different in many families, and parents are there from the outset, ready with advice. At Middlebury this is clear during registration for new students. Although registration can easily be done online, by design it's held the old-fashioned way, with professors gathered in the school's hockey arena, sitting at tables that represent their department. As the students learn which courses they have gotten into—or didn't—they are all supposed to take their questions to the waiting professors.

But it doesn't happen that way anymore.

Instead many students pull out their cell phones and a chorus of laments rises up from this remote New England sports rink to reach hundreds of parents scattered across the globe (including some just leaving the college's parking lot): "If I can't get into organic chemistry should I take biology?"

The students could talk to their academic advisors, since they have just met with them the day before on the very same issue of course selections. But in the world of iConnected parenting this too is increasingly unlikely to happen. The tie between parent and child is tight, and constant communication is pulling the cord tighter. In recent years college parents have been told to just "let go." But as we all learned from the Reagan era of Just Say No, counting on slogans to bring about profound social change doesn't work. Many parents have spent years helping their students get into college, supervising their school work, and carting them to countless résumé-building activities. Once the goal of college is achieved, many parents aren't sure how much to stay involved. The instant access of cell phones and computers reinforces their uncertainty. How can I let go when I can talk to my child almost instantly, anywhere, anytime? And besides, I *want* to talk to my child, and my child wants to talk to me, and everyone else is doing it too!

The level of parents' involvement in their child's college experience is rising. Just letting go is not the solution, and many parents know that intuitively. After dropping off Buck's older brother at college, his mother said, "I was a wreck. I even got the book *Letting Go*. But it didn't help. I cried all the way home." Since then she and her husband have also sent Buck and another son to college. "It didn't get any easier for me. We are a very close family. I didn't feel any different when any one of them left home."

The kids recognize the incongruity of their parents' ability to stay in touch whenever they want. For one student at Grinnell College in Iowa, this became evident during the college's orientation for first-year students and their families: "They make this symbolic ceremony of separating parents from kids under a big arch. I remember my mom crying under the arch and she was bawling and bawling, and then she called me later that night. They have this big farewell goodbye ceremony—and then most people talk to each other that day."

One giant upside to iConnected parenting (and potentially its most powerful downside) is the closeness between parent and child. The key to any child's developing a healthy emotional, psychological independence is for parents to maintain that close connection while at the same time giving the child enough space to grow. For college students it is also key to have parents who *stay in touch while letting them grow*. This can be much harder for parents to figure out how to do, given the pressure to stay involved and the potential for 24/7 contact. But we hope to help you rise to the challenge.

In our research and reporting we have discovered that iConnected parenting is deeply affecting students academically, socially, and professionally. It is influencing how they experience college, and even the years after that. It is shaping how they feel about themselves and their parents, and it shapes how others view them. In the long run, for many young people iConnected parenting is putting their passage to adulthood on indefinite hold.

It doesn't have to be this way.

There are ways to successfully navigate this world of close connections, to help young people get the most out of college, grow into competent adults, and feel authentically good about themselves and their parents. That is what this book is about.

## Chapter 2

# The Electronic Tether  - - - - - - - - - - - - - - - -

## Communication between Today's College Students and Their Parents

*"This was hard," says Annie, as she hands her advisor a draft of her honors thesis. It's tough to imagine anything being hard for Annie. An athlete at an elite Division III college, she has just returned from a challenging semester studying abroad. Annie explains why it was so difficult: "It's the first time in my college career that I know so much more about a topic than my dad does." It's also the first paper that Annie, a senior in college, has done without her dad's editing help. She seems proud to have finally crossed that threshold, to recognize that she is capable of doing her own work without his help.*

As stories like this surface at campuses across the country it has become clear that many students, not just Annie, are using email, cell phones, iPhones, BlackBerrys, computers, Skype, and whatever new technology they can find to connect with their parents on issues large and small and to get their help. And they are connecting a lot. If you are a parent of a college student you might wonder whether you should be emailing and calling your child so frequently. College students are supposed to be more independent than they were in high school. Before cell phones became a fact of life, college kids had to be more self-reliant.

## The Transition to College

The first research study at Middlebury began with the simple goal of finding out what happens to communication with parents when students first head off to college. The initial questions, posed in focus groups and online surveys, were basic. To students preparing to enter college we asked: How much do you expect to talk to your parents when you go to college? At the end of their first semester we asked the same students: How much do you actually talk to your parents now that you're in college?

Before arriving at college, students predicted that they would be talking to their parents (in any form: cell phone, email, etc.), on average, *once a week*. This was in line with what many middle-aged adults, now parents of these students, recalled from their own college experience. We also found that most students hadn't actually discussed with their parents how often they'd talk. They'd just made assumptions, which they imagined their parents shared.

Focus groups in the summer showed that recent high school grads looked forward to a life with less contact with mom and dad. They talked excitedly about leaving home, getting to make decisions on their own, and no longer answering to parents on a daily basis. As one son proudly reported, "I'm trying to have a realization with my parents that they're not always going to be the support system, the control system. I'm trying to create my own support system." This confirmed our early assumption: students envisioned college as a parent-free zone and an important step in growing up, an altogether exhilarating prospect. They believed that, once they set foot on campus, these changes would happen overnight. Based on all of this, their assumption of a weekly call seemed reasonable to them.

The results of the follow-up to the first survey study radically contradicted the students' predictions. Surveys of the same students at the end of the first semester showed that they were in touch with their parents an average of *10.4 times per week*, far more than they (or we researchers) had anticipated. Also surprising was the reaction of the Middlebury students working on the research team, who were only a few years older than the survey participants: the student researchers themselves were shocked by how much had changed during their years in college. Elena Kennedy, a senior whose work on this research became her honors thesis, didn't have much of an attachment to her cell phone when she arrived at Middlebury in the fall of 2002, and much of her class was similar in this respect, if they had cell phones at all. Elena commented, "We didn't carry them around campus with us then." She was surprised that by the time she was a senior the arriving freshmen saw cell phones as indispensable and were seen talking on them everywhere, a significant change in campus culture, and an annoying one to many outgoing seniors.

Most important, when Elena's class began college in 2002 very few parents used cell phones regularly. As cell phones blanketed the college market and then the parent market, a communications revolution between college kids and their parents occurred.

This revolution brought about substantial change, and we wondered how well this new generation of students was adapting to it. For starters, wouldn't it be depressing for a student to expect all that independence and then, once he got on campus, still be connecting with his parents every day? We thought so, but the data told another story. Most students weren't unhappy about it at all—even though there was a huge discrepancy between their expectations and the reality of what was happening during that first semester. This was a fascinating, if somewhat disturbing, finding.

## Parent Involvement Continues in College

The fundamental question remained: How healthy is such frequent contact? The surveys given to the same students both before college and at the end of the first semester in 2005 revealed reason for concern. Parents who closely managed their kids during high school—reminding them to study for a test, clean their rooms, write papers that were due—were at it again in college, abetted by cell phones and email. Parental supervision that might have naturally ebbed when an adolescent left home now continued during the first term.

The students gave examples of how their parents were involved in their lives in unprecedented ways. In a focus group of a dozen students, conducted at the end of the first year of college, one young man admitted that his mom had copies of all four of his course syllabi and called regularly to remind him of due dates and to check on his progress. ("Have you started the paper for European History that's due on Friday?") None of the other freshmen in the room acted as if this were unusual. Meanwhile those of us running the focus group struggled not to show our concern about the young man's

17

casual accounting of his mom's over-the-top involvement. By now, developmentally, he should have been managing his own studies and asserting his independence from mom. Equally alarming was how readily the other students viewed his mom's behavior as perfectly natural. Even the college seniors on our research team were stunned about "this new generation" and their dependency on their parents.

This kind of behavior was rare before cell phones, unlimited calling plans, and the involved parent culture. Our professional concerns about the psychological impact of this emerging "electronic tether" continued to deepen. Having heard the anecdotal buzz about "soccer moms" and "helicopter parents," journalists then began to report on the research. *Newsweek,* for example, covered the Middlebury results in a 2006 story titled "The Fine Art of Letting Go," and the research was cited throughout 2006 and 2007 in the *New York Times*, the *Washington Post*, the *Christian Science Monitor*, the *Wall Street Journal*, and other publications. Clearly we professionals weren't alone in our concerns about this new trend.

## Communication with Parents during the College Years

As news of the survey spread, some burning questions began to emerge. Was all this talk between parents and kids something that just happens in the first semester of college? Was it something that only families at elite liberal arts colleges did? Was it just another case of the helicopter crowd going berserk?

It was time to dig deeper. So we surveyed the same students at the end of their second semester. Perhaps contact with home would have dropped off as homesickness abated and kids learned to make decisions on their own. But it hadn't. Parents and kids were still chatting away. In a third study, developed by senior Katie Hurd, we found that even students who had taken a semester off before attending college (to travel or work or do an internship) were still in constant touch with mom and dad. We thought they might be more independent, given the time away from home on their own, but that too proved false.

Julia, for example, spent a fall abroad before matriculating at college her first year. She learned to manage her own time, money, and life, along with a new relationship. She talked to her parents only occasionally. She felt like an adult! But that changed once she arrived at college. Now her mom, in California, calls every day. An exasperated Julia explains why: "Because, she says, 'I spent eighteen years knowing everything about your life! Why would I want to stop now?'" Meanwhile the daily calls about family life and drama have increased Julia's homesickness, which is now worse during her sophomore year at college than when she was a continent away two years ago. Julia says she feels like less of an adult at 20 than she did at 18. Parents who call too frequently are providing constant reminders of home in ways that can prolong homesickness rather than alleviating it.

This constant connection to home was more pervasive than we had expected and also appeared to have some genuine disadvantages. To get to the heart of this phenomenon, Barbara and thesis student Nancy Fullman enlarged the study and, in the fall of 2006, launched a new survey of nearly a thousand students and their parents, this time at both Middlebury and the University of Michigan. Large, public, and in the Midwest, Michigan provided a different perspective from Middlebury's. The new survey was designed to explore students' contact with parents across all four years of college and examine whether all this talking was an isolated phenomenon or was exaggerated at a private liberal arts college. We also wanted to make the surveys as relevant as possible, so students on the research team drew from their own experiences to help develop the questions, and we ran more focus groups to make sure we were tapping student perceptions fully in the kinds of questions we asked.

## How Often Are College Students Talking to Their Parents?

Our new survey respondents dashed our expectations once again. We had thought that, if college students stayed in constant touch with their parents throughout their first year, perhaps the decline came later. Maybe the calls and emails would drop off as students grew more confident about their own decision making, study skills, and independent lives. But we found quite the opposite.

The average number of times that families communicated was *13.4 times per week.*

It didn't matter what year students were in school. Whether they were sophomores or seniors, they all talked about the same amount of time, mostly on cell phones (owned by 97 percent of students in the study), followed by email. Students at both schools stayed in contact with their parents at about the same rate (13.5 times per week at Middlebury and 13.2 at Michigan). Later, Abby's reporting based on interviews with students, parents, administrators, and faculty members at schools around the country showed a similar pattern, with minimal variations. So this wasn't a geographic or small private college trend after all; iConnected parenting was a growing national phenomenon.

In addition it doesn't appear to be have subsided since then. A 2008 follow-up study of the Middlebury and Michigan students, conducted with Middlebury thesis student Catherine Timmins, showed that contacts with parents continued to average just over 13 times a week.

## Who's Making All These Calls? (It's Not Just the Parents)

The Middlebury-Michigan study also crushed the assumption that parents were driving this new behavior. Kids were speed-dialing mom and dad almost as much as their parents were calling them. Considering that students themselves were reporting this behavior, it is likely that they might underreport it and very unlikely that they would be exaggerating it.

The mutuality of the contact was surprising. The media coverage seemed to suggest that hovering parents weren't willing to let go and were simply descending uninvited into students' lives, but that wasn't the case. Students were willing to accept and even invite their parents into their college lives. For example, one upbeat student described her communications from just the previous week—a call with mom to talk about auditions for a musical group, an email about news from home, a call to dad to get advice about course registration, and then a call with mom about dorm issues—and the list continued. This frequent back and forth, the routine recounting of daily life, and the seeking of advice from parents now seemed to be, for many, a natural extension of family life into the college years, no matter the distance apart.

Again and again throughout our later interviews students who at first downplayed their own contact with parents would often raise their initial figures, supporting the survey findings. A college junior from the West Coast heard the results of the survey and said it seemed outrageous, given that she talked to her mom "only" about three times a week. "Who are these people?" she asked disdainfully. Her tone changed, though, as she revised her estimates aloud: "Oh, but my dad does call me every day on his way to work, and we all email. So I guess it does fit."

In only a few years this continuous contact—a cultural sea change—has become commonplace for many families. Students themselves seem unaware of just how connected they are and what this might mean for their own growth and independence, or how different their college experience is even from that of their older siblings (or their parents!).

**Table 1. Frequency of Communication between
College Students and Their Parents**

| Year | Weekly contacts | Parent / student initiated |
|---|---|---|
| First-years | 13.4 | 7.1 / 6.3 |
| Sophomores | 13.2 | 7.0 / 6.2 |
| Juniors | 14.1 | 7.3 / 6.8 |
| Seniors | 13.0 | 7.0 / 6.0 |

## Student Differences

The averages in Table 1 describe what's normative; not everyone talks that much, and the data show considerable variability among the students. Some were proud of sticking to the weekly call and occasional email. Take Will, for instance, a sophomore at the University of Connecticut, whom Abby met during her reporting. "I lived with my parents for eighteen years. I don't need to talk to them every day now!" he said. In fact he said, "It was mom's idea to call at least once a week." Even then, he won't take her call immediately if he's hanging out with friends, studying, or eating. His reason: "She won't let me get off the phone." Instead he calls her back when it's more convenient for him and other people aren't around.

Some students do tease their peers who can't go a day without a call to or from mom and dad. Will's friend Tim, whose parents are divorced, calls both families (mom and stepdad, father and sister) every night. Tim's freshman roommate asked him repeatedly, "Why are you always calling your family?" Many students talk frequently to mom and dad, but some of those who talk the most are quickly marked by their peers. Some are made fun of outright, while others feel a hint of disapproval.

We also found dramatic extremes, including a few kids who were estranged from their parents and didn't want much contact at all. On the other end of the scale were students who needed frequent reassuring contact. Some of these were driven by concerns that were clinical in nature (students struggling with depression, for example). Others were going through rough patches of academic difficulty, loneliness, or personal confusion.

The research team expected to find aspects of students' backgrounds that might predict their level of communication. By design, students in the survey were a diverse group, varying in all sorts of interesting and important ways. We thought that a student's ethnic background or parents' income might affect the level of communication. But we found no differences—not by income, ethnicity, race, or distance from home. Maybe if they had gone to boarding school they became independent earlier? No, not according to our data. As one student noted, "I talk to them more now than I did at boarding school because now I have more time." The relatively unstructured nature of college gives students choices about their time, and some are eager to fill it, perhaps unaccustomed to the freedom of their new schedule. After a lifetime of overscheduling, all this free time makes some students uncomfortable; now, with just a few hours of class each day, they have to figure out how to fill the rest of their day. Phone calls to parents who are always willing to listen can easily fill the void. One mother told Abby, "Whenever [my daughter] was bored, I was her entertainment. If she was waiting for someone outside to have lunch or when she got to practice early or between breakfast and class, I'm her entertainment."

Only the sex of the child made a difference in frequency of communication, although not as much as expected. Daughters talked more to their parents than sons did: 14.5 compared to 11.3 times per week. On average both male and female students talked more with mom than dad—a pattern likely begun in childhood—and daughters even more so. A quarter of the students reported talking equally to both parents, and male students reported that this was more likely to be the case (37 percent vs. 20 percent).

## How Satisfied Are the Students with So Much Communication?

About 75 percent of the students surveyed seemed happy with how much they talked to their parents. Remarkably those who were dissatisfied were likely to want *more* talk, not less. On the extreme end, one student commented on the survey, "It's hard to get everything in a simple telephone conversation. If there was a way to meet for coffee every day and chat, then things would be perfect." People who went to college a generation ago are not likely to recall wishing they could have met mom and dad at their version of Starbucks every day to process their college experience.

This is a radical change, and from a psychological viewpoint, it's also of concern. Some students voiced their own worries: "I actually feel like I contact my parents too much, not the other way around." Parents can help students make this transition by not being always available. That way their kids will have the space and motivation to make new friends at college. The danger of mom as "best friend" is that a child doesn't have as much need for a new friendship with a peer, which takes effort to develop. If kids are busy chatting a couple of times a day with mom, they also have less time to find potential friends.

Yet for some kids even all this talking isn't enough, particularly when it comes to dads. More than a quarter of the students in the study (27 percent) expressed a desire to talk more often with dad; daughters in particular (33 percent) wanted more connection. Moms might want to consider handing over the phone more often to dad or encouraging him to initiate some calls himself.

**Table 2. Student Satisfaction with Parent Contact, in percentages**

| | Contact with Mother | | | Contact with Father | | |
|---|---|---|---|---|---|---|
| | Want less | Satisfied | Want more | Want less | Satis-fied | Want more |
| Females (n=578) | 7 | 77 | 16 | 4 | 63 | 33 |
| Males (n=319) | 4 | 80 | 16 | 3 | 76 | 21 |

Although most students were content with how often they connect with their parents, *they didn't feel that their satisfaction was shared by their parents.* More than half the students believed their parents wanted even more contact.

**Table 3. Student Perceptions of Parental Satisfaction with Contact, in percentages**

| | Perceptions of Mother's Satisfaction | | | Perceptions of Father's Satisfaction | | |
|---|---|---|---|---|---|---|
| | Want less | Satisfied | Want more | Want less | Satisfied | Want more |
| Females | 3 | 46 | 52 | 3 | 43 | 54 |
| Males | 2 | 36 | 62 | 1 | 56 | 43 |

## How *Do* Parents Feel?

Eager to get parents' perspectives, we added a parent survey to the mix. Although students might be surprised to learn this, most parents (70 percent) were in fact generally satisfied with how much they talked to their kids and typically didn't want more contact, or at least not to the degree that students thought they did. One father of a senior woman commented, "We love our kids dearly, but do not believe we should go along with them to college via cell phone and Internet (aka 'electronic leashes'!). We are glad to have open dialogue with them on most every topic; however, we tend to respond rather than initiate, in an attempt to keep contact from being too frequent. I also try hard to avoid offering unsolicited advice. For us, no news is typically good news." Still, a sizable group of parents (29 percent) did want more communication. The mother of a freshman said about her daughter's lack of contact, "We gently remind her that we would like to hear from her more often."

Kids are often aware of their parents' desire for more contact, but some become so absorbed in their college experience that they don't have the time or inclination to meet it. At Grinnell College, which prides itself on its close-knit community, one student told Abby, "When I came to Grinnell, the first week or so I called every day, maybe more than once. Then the community kind of sucked me in and I became so involved with activities and friends and schoolwork that the focus of my life kind of shifted from my life at home into my life at Grinnell. Now I definitely talk to them several times per week, maybe twice (along with an occasional email or text). I am fully aware that my family would like more. And it's been hard for my friends [outside of Grinnell] and family. There's something that Grinnell offers me that other people can't."

This healthy attitude about forging her own life while staying in contact, but neither incessantly nor with too much dependence, isn't shared by her midwestern hometown friends, scattered at schools across the country. Their reaction to her amount of contact underscores how pervasive parental contact really is. "They've been surprised when they found out that I don't talk to my parents every day. They are like, 'Are you serious?'"

Parents, however, seldom seem to want less contact; only 1 percent of those in our study did. Nor are they particularly aware that their kids might want less (also 1 percent). Some parents, however, even if they were satisfied overall, worried that there were times when their kids were calling too often. One father expressed the basis for his concern: "It's just that there's so much more communication than we had with our parents when we were in school. I just wondered if he was connecting with his peers very well." Overall most parents (88 percent) believe that their kids are happy with how much they connect; only 11 percent believe their kids might want even more.

It seems critically important for parents and their children to learn to talk about how much contact is enough, and to become sensitive to when the calls are coming too frequently. Parents might consider backing off a bit and letting their child take time to explore new relationships. Socializing in a new environment isn't easy work for some college students, and is seldom as easy as calling parents with concerns, but in the long run it's the healthier path.

## What Are They Talking About?

With all this conversation back and forth—calls, emails, text messages, and the increasingly rare letter or card—we thought it important to find out what students and their parents are talking about. At the most general level, some topics are family staples. Academic talk is common, but these conversations range from the terse ("Fine.") and mundane ("I wish my Spanish class weren't at eight a.m.") to the sublime ("I went to a poetry reading last night and I think it changed my life!"), with doses of whining ("I can't possibly finish all my reading this week!" or "My econ class sucks.") and help seeking ("I can't think of anything to write about for the Intro Psych paper due tomorrow! Got any ideas?"). Daily life—discussion of roommates, sports, social life—and finances, of course, also appear to be conversational mainstays with parents throughout the undergraduate experience. Parents in the study spoke of the pleasure of being allowed inside this world. One Middlebury mother said, "[My son's] life is so interesting and stimulating. I have loved hearing about his classes, like hearing about a good play or event. He is a good storyteller and has given us little glimpses into college life."

Other topics change with both the rhythm of the semester and year in school and the growing maturity of the student. Asked when they might talk to their parents more than usual, students reported two extremes: they call home when they are most stressed and need to vent or when they are bored or have sudden bursts of free time. Others describe some of these calls as "filler," something to do en route to class or in the lull before dinner. One student summed it up this way: "I only call on my way to the gym. That way I can say, 'Gotta go now, I'm here!'"

Students also talk to their parents more when they are planning a trip home or have a decision to make, large or small. In an earlier era students likely would have conferred with parents on major decisions and finances, but today's students are routinely consulting their parents on such matters as how to cook potatoes, change a tire, do laundry, and choose courses or paper topics.

Sometimes this frequent advice seeking suggests that students are overly reliant on parents, but at times it can be a gesture to include parents in their lives. Elena Kennedy, the student whose thesis helped launch this research, called her mom before participating in a formal presentation about the study during her senior year to ask, "Should I dress as a college student or as a professional?" She knew what answer her mom would give ("Professional!"); that was her choice as well. But the conversation gave Elena a way to let her mother share in the excitement of a meaningful event. Others, however, may find that their ability to make their own decisions (as limited as it may be in some cases) begins to atrophy. One student, a sophomore, attended Barbara's presentation about the study's results and decided to act on the findings. He described in an email to her how liberating it was to decide which course to take in the upcoming winter term, a four-week intensive when students take just one elective course, without consulting his mom. It was the first time he had done so.

We recommend that parents whose kids routinely call them about such decisions wait before offering advice. Instead, actively listen, and encourage your child to find the appropriate resources on campus (a professor or academic advisor or friend) to help her make her own decisions.

Each year of college brings new sets of challenges and decisions, as has always been the case, and our survey revealed changes in advice seeking over the four years. First-year students were most likely to request academic help from parents (and it's presumably easier for most parents to give help in an introductory course than an advanced one). One big decision all students make is choosing a major, generally sometime during their first two years, although the timing varies by institution. For many sophomores the issue of study abroad arises.

Most students reported that their parents became involved in these milestones—in some cases, too much so. Some noted that their parents encouraged them to choose a major that the student found interesting and enjoyable ("They just want me to be happy"); others spoke of their parents' guidance to choose a major with potential for financial gain. Although it might seem reasonable for parents to suggest considering future income when choosing a major, these expectations can negatively affect their children, some of whom will be unhappy with the coursework required. For example, students described plodding through economics courses that hold no interest for them but that are supposedly a path to success.

At some colleges the number of students declaring double majors has soared, and many students report that they have one major for their parents and another for themselves. One double major in theater and psychology talked about how unhappy his parents would have been had he majored only in theater, but he didn't want to give it up; not surprisingly, however, the strain of doing both was taking its toll. Parents might want to listen carefully when their kids report their plan for a double major and ask them why; they might be trying to live up to their parents' expectations. They might also want to ask themselves whether the stress associated with the heavy commitment required to do a double major is worth it for their child. Many students we talked to are highly sensitive to the current economic climate and want to please the adults who are paying the tuition bills, but they are sometimes deferring their own dreams to do so.

In our student survey data we found that by junior year many students report discussing with their parents the possibility of internships or summer jobs that are helpful for career choices; by senior year the prospect of a job or graduate school looms, as well as issues of relocating, and once again parents offer advice. Discussions of practical career issues appear to increase each year throughout college, and dramatically so between junior and senior year, when discussion of future plans also takes a leap. As a sign of the times, one Michigan student noted, "My father said to make sure I get a job I'm good at and that pays well instead of one I would enjoy more but pays less. He's right—in the end money and power are really all that matters."

For the most part, students respect their parents' advice, especially when they have actually asked for it. But students don't always ask, and it's understandable that parents would fall back on old habits, so that "Eat your vegetables" becomes "Don't forget you need sleep before that test tomorrow." More than one student noted that this kind of admonishment wasn't welcome: "I don't usually ask for their advice, but that doesn't stop them from giving it." Some joked that the advice was the same regardless of the crisis du jour. One student said, "My dad's general advice is 'This will pass, just try to get some sleep and relax.'" Students seemed to most appreciate advice when they asked for it and when their parents had some expertise in the issue, but they don't appreciate advice that seems meddling. One student moaned, "My mom likes to give advice about relationships, no matter what." Parents who wait until asked their opinion before giving it are likely to find conversations that grow over time toward more depth and reciprocity.

As students begin to inquire about how their parents are doing, conversations become less one-sided. Upper-level students are more likely to report conversations about their parents' lives and work. Each year the conversations include more talk of brothers and sisters, as growing maturity makes it possible for students to weigh in on issues at home. Most students place boundaries around their conversations with parents, but some say they talk about "everything," and they really do mean *everything*, including vivid descriptions of sex, parties, and drinking binges. Even those who aren't that open are more candid in their discussions than most parents remember being with their own parents.

As our research shows, today's college students are in frequent and regular contact with their parents, even though they hadn't planned to be. Few families discuss before the kids leave home when or how to communicate during the college years. In addition, despite all the time on the phone and email, there seems to be little talk among families about how they actually feel about so much communication. And misperceptions abound. Students are talking twice a day to mom and dad and thinking that their parents want even more, which doesn't appear to be the case. We encourage parents of freshmen to have a conversation before the big trip to campus in September about

31

what would be best—for the student. Ask your child how often he would like to talk. Setting a regular time to catch up can also be beneficial, even when there are short emails, calls, or texts sprinkled into the week.

"Is all this communication good or bad?" we're often asked. Well, it depends, of course. In the next chapter we talk about the implications for students' psychological development.

## Chapter 3

# Can College Kids Grow Up on an Electronic Tether?

When many students arrive at college, they expect to finally be able to call the shots in their own lives. Not that they won't miss their parents, but they look forward to the freedom college represents, deciding what to do and when to do it. But in our focus groups, interviews, and surveys, we learned that well into college many students are getting the same reminders from home: study, please clean your room, and don't forget to write that paper! New items get added to the list: Have you filed the study abroad form? The internship application? Some students feel like they can't make a move on their own. And college? It just isn't the experience that they expected or wanted.

Others make their parents part of their daily lives, calling home with the latest: practices, games, grades, professors, parties. These calls are an almost seamless continuation of the conversations they had regularly at the kitchen table after school. This is the way it is and always has been for some students. Many call mom—sometimes even dad—"a best friend."

The continuous connection between home and campus is trans-

33

forming the college experience, and our research and reporting make that clear. We wanted to know how all this contact with mom and dad is affecting the development of students on the threshold of adulthood. Despite the rising prevalence of cell phones, email, texting, Skype, and unlimited calling and data plans, we were surprised to find how little this subject has been studied.

## Developing Autonomy

Our first big question was: What happens to the independence of college students who are in constant contact with their parents? So we designed our surveys to also capture as much as possible about students' psychological development, their parents' involvement in their lives, and their relationships with their parents.

In the past it was easy for college students to choose how much contact they had with their parents, and parents seemed to expect less. Because contact was typically fairly limited, students quickly got a taste of making their own decisions—about courses, drugs, sex— and they reveled in that freedom. (Back then parents didn't always know what their children were doing, and perhaps it was easier for parents that way.) Not surprisingly, past research showed that this freedom of choice and independence led to improved relationships with parents after the kids left home. No longer in the daily scrum of curfews, homework, and household chores, college students were freed from conflicts. The kind of arguments common in high school ("Mom! Mandy doesn't have a curfew, so how come *I* have to be in at eleven?") vanished. Away from home and on their own, students used this time to learn to separate and to make increasingly more of their own decisions. Maybe they stumbled along the way, but they grew to adulthood in the process.

Not so much anymore.

34

## A Crash Course in Becoming Independent

One of the key tasks that begins in adolescence and continues into adulthood is to learn to become one's own person. This doesn't mean, of course, cutting ties with family. On the contrary, it means finding a balance between independence and connection to family. Autonomous young people are able to make decisions about their own lives and take responsibility for their behavior, and they can do this best in the context of a strong and loving connection with their parents. As one of the students in our study put it, "I have realized what an important part of my life my parents are. At first I was very excited to get away from home and be on my own, but now breaking away from home is not very important. I know my parents are always there for me, and as a result I want to keep them in my life." Being separate while staying connected, rather than breaking away, is the ideal, and kids need room to find this out for themselves. They need to have enough space apart to learn for themselves that they do want to have their parents in their lives. Without the freedom to separate and make this discovery, resentments that arose during high school can continue to simmer, along with the desire to break away.

There seems little doubt that most parents want their growing children to become independent, and that the children want it too. College personnel—faculty, administrators, student and residential life staff—expect students to be moving toward these goals and are prepared to help them get there. Unfortunately parents thwart this process through overinvolvement in the college years, which is often preceded by overinvolvement in the high school years. Sometimes this is fed by a well-meaning desire to help and then is reinforced by short-term gains. A common example is editing a son's paper so that he earns a better grade. But in the long run this kind of behavior impedes healthy development.

Psychologists view autonomy as a basic human need across the life

35

span. We adults know that we are much more motivated when we get a say at work and have a voice in things that matter to us, whether it's choosing a project or a day off. The same goes for adolescents. Selecting a topic for a paper or deciding when to do chores at home can be motivating. And yet adults (parents and teachers) sometimes ignore the fact that the same conditions that motivate us also motivate our kids. Think of the student who believed college would allow him to finally live his own life, but who now feels as though he's a puppet with strings being pulled via cell phone. It's hard for him to care or to get excited about the work when he's not really doing it for himself.

Young people at college face dozens of decisions every day: when to sleep, what to eat, whether to hit a Thursday night party before a Friday morning class. They need the right kind of support from parents and other caring adults as they make choices that their parents once decided for them. Learning to make responsible choices doesn't happen overnight, and it takes practice. Larger decisions also loom, about friends and relationships, majors, summer plans, and time abroad. Personal choices about drinking, cutting class, attending religious services, and completing assignments are part of the independence of college.

All these choices shape a person and help form the identity and sense of self that will carry your son or daughter into adulthood—if he or she actually gets to make these decisions. Today, though, a good number of parents want to be part of this decision-making process, and many are. Often they believe they are protecting their child and a substantial investment too, given the high cost of college. Yet in the past students worked through most of these decisions with friends and others at college rather than with their parents. They became their own person by learning to make these decisions with multiple sounding boards.

The pressure to become autonomous doesn't suddenly crop up at age 18. It starts in early adolescence. Most parents recall in painful detail the first indicator they got of their child's move toward independence; it's what psychologists call *de-idealizing* the parents. Remember the first time your child was uncomfortable being seen with you? Or groaned and rolled her eyes when you sang along on the radio with the Beatles or Sting or Garth Brooks? Childhood was over. Being knocked off your pedestal might have hurt, but it was part of an adolescent's positive growth toward being a separate person. Other signs of this move toward autonomy will also be acutely familiar: "Do I have to go on vacation with the *family*? Can't I take a friend?" That's when adolescents see themselves as separate from the family. The ability to make independent choices is another sign of maturity, along with learning to see parents as people with lives and interests of their own, not just as mom and dad.

This final change—seeing parents as people—usually happens in late adolescence or early adulthood. It might surface during one of those calls from home, when a once self-occupied teen suddenly asks, "But, Mom, how was *your* day?" or asks about *your* childhood. Our research showed older students making progress in this area, but younger students were not. Sometimes this ability to see others as autonomous works both ways, as one dad observed in a parent orientation session: "I don't know how my son views *me*, but my struggle is to learn to see *him* as a separate person!" Over time, though, these steps in autonomy come together in ways that foster a refreshing, adult-to-adult relationship.

Learning to be a separate person within the family isn't always easy, of course. The development of independent beliefs and values may be a struggle. In some cases it means that students accept many of their parents' values after critical examination; in others it means pulling away from family beliefs. For example, many students begin to question and reexamine the religion in which they were raised. As a freshman at Penn, Abby stopped attending Sunday Mass. Her decision disturbed her parents, especially her dad, who was a devout Irish

Catholic. ("Just say a prayer" was one of his favorite sayings when Abby shared her worries with him.) Abby was very close to her dad, and upsetting him made her uncomfortable, but she didn't agree with all of the Church's teachings. Wisely her parents chose not to push the matter. Eventually Abby sorted out her issues with the Church on her own and went back to attending Mass. Barbara remembers arriving home one Thanksgiving and explaining a bit nervously that she was now a vegetarian. Her mother responded with curiosity, good questions, and support, but without judgment. These types of choices and experiments are common in the college years, and how parents respond is critical.

Students in our study described some of their struggles in coming to terms with their own values. Observed one senior, "I've realized that my parents are people too, and they can make mistakes and may not automatically know what's right for me. I'm currently making the shift from being motivated by their expectations of me to being motivated by my own values, which has resulted in a bit of friction. I tend to be quietly irritable when I'm around them because I'm very critical of what they've taught me to believe." Another senior offered a more positive spin: "I think that my parents respect me as an adult and enjoy my companionship more (now that I am out of the house!). We actually disagree more now, due to my growing independence and development of my own personal beliefs and values, however they are very open to sharing those disagreements. Sometimes we argue over them, but rarely in anger. In high school, this mutual respect did not exist as much." Parents who make room for these conversations and allow for the discussion of differences are likely to find that their relationship with their child blossoms during this period. Some students learn the hard way that it's not okay to question their parents' values and that their new opinions are not treated with respect. This might not keep them from questioning or from holding new beliefs, but it can keep them from discussing them with their parents.

Overall researchers have found that college students who learn to take charge of their lives and think for themselves without their parents hovering overhead are more likely to achieve better grades and more fulfilling careers after college. This progression toward autonomy is a long road, but one worth supporting. Knowing this may help parents avoid the temptation to rush in and fix things. The hardest part may be allowing your children to make mistakes. Permitting the occasional stumble, what clinical psychologist Wendy Mogel calls "the blessing of a skinned knee," is just as important during college as during childhood in building self-reliance.

## Our Research Findings

*Tethered Students Are Slow to Grow Up*
Based on our extensive surveys of Middlebury and Michigan students, the bottom line is that *students who have the most frequent contact with their parents are less autonomous than other students.* They are least likely to have achieved some of the psychological benchmarks of independence that in the past would have been typical of this age, according to standard psychological tests included in the surveys. This is deeply troubling.

We are concerned about these findings because independence is especially important at this age. Students who are low in autonomy have a hard time functioning on their own. They may depend on wake-up calls, reminders that work is due, and a nudge to think ahead about summer plans. They are more likely to rely on their parents emotionally than students who aren't talking to their parents as much. These students are less capable of independent thinking and decision making. They also don't view their parents as individuals, with lives apart from their roles as parents, and may expect their parents' lives to still be centered around their parenting roles. As one

39

student observed, "Right now my parents are on vacation in California, and it is strange they are occupied by something other than *me.*" There is a sense of entitlement driving these expectations, with students assuming that parents devote all of their time and energy to them. In the process, appreciation for what parents actually do can become a casualty. Not surprisingly these students' continued need to be the center of mom and dad's universe goes hand in hand with their inability to take ownership of their own beliefs and values. If they can't see their parents as having a life apart from them, it's hard to develop their own standards. These are the kids who can't yet think for themselves and haven't analyzed issues and ideas on their own. Rather than carefully reviewing the pros and cons of each presidential candidate on their own, for example, they simply vote for whomever their parents prefer. Their values are still copies rather than deeply reflected and hard-won parts of their own sense of their adult self. They don't see their views or their own lives as separate from those of their parents.

We don't know, of course, whether constantly communicating with their parents stunts their independence, or whether all the talking is because they are so dependent on their parents. We do know that high contact and low autonomy are connected, so the dependency can now continue unabated, fueled by cell phones and email.

The years spent in college are particularly important because this is usually the first time kids are away from home and on their own for an extended period and aren't planning to return to the nest full time afterward. College isn't like going away to camp at age 12, although some parents seem to regard it that way. This is the juncture in the transition to adulthood, to moving on in the world and making one's own way. The support provided by most colleges and universities means that this transition is not a shove out of the nest, but a place to experience a gradual progression to independence, with peers and caring adults who can assist in the process.

*Decision Making in College: Who's Calling the Shots?*
Students in our surveys said they are making the big decisions mostly by themselves. That being said, they *also* said they are talking to their parents about those decisions and getting tons of advice and pressure to match. Many parents are wary of a major that won't lead to immediate and secure employment, and they let their children know it. Students reported parent comments such as "Is philosophy good for anything?" and "English—you better get a teacher's certificate too." And Italian, well, according to one student's parents, "Italian = uselessness. Econ = useful." Or at least that's what the student heard.

Business was the most prominent choice of major for the 2008 entering class of freshmen at four-year colleges, according to a national survey of the University of California at Los Angeles Higher Education Research Institute, and it seems to be mom and dad's favorite major too. At Michigan only two of the students in the study reported that their parents had tried to steer them away from economics or business, although there were many stories of being pressured to shift *toward* these fields. One student reported that he switched his psychology major to economics to please his parents, because they had made it clear that "they wanted a 'business-like' major." Some students lamented the loss of their own interests. Faculty members lament teaching students who aren't excited about their majors and who are abandoning their passions.

Many students reported that their parents commented about employment prospects and finances in general: "How I would 'use' my major [was a concern]" and "They were worried I wouldn't be able to 'do' anything with my major after college."

Not all parents were described as heavy-handed. Some offered advice but left the decision up to the student: "They cautioned me that I'd be broke throughout my twenties although they strongly encouraged the major [environmental studies] because it's my passion." Some students happily reported that their parents supported and respected their choices. These responses were rare, but often exuberant: "They told me that if I choose to do what I love to do, then I will never 'work' a day in my life. I am a jazz performance major, and they have been completely supportive."

The pressure to choose a career that pleases parents isn't new, but technology-savvy parents are intervening in new ways and with more frequency. They check out deadlines for major declaration on the college's website, call their kids to discuss their choices, and lobby in regular calls. These same parents might have trouble imagining a similar scenario during their own college years.

Parents' concerns about their children's ability to support themselves after college are certainly understandable, especially in the current economy. But the pressure to please their parents with a pragmatic career path puts students in a classic catch-22: if they don't follow their parents' advice, they will disappoint their parents; if they do follow their parents' advice, they might not enjoy their studies and college experience as much as if they had followed their heart.

You might want to consider the approach taken by the parents of Buck, a student at the University of Minnesota. Midway through college Buck changed his major from the ever-practical sciences to the more nebulous major of communications, a choice that he discussed frequently with his parents. In the end, though, says Buck, "It was entirely my decision." He feels very good about this new major—it's really where his heart is. But that change has meant a substantial tuition increase to cover the cost of courses needed to satisfy his new major's requirements. The financial consequences of Buck's choice affected him and his family. His parents make a decent income, but they are not in the ranks of the upper affluent. Both Buck and his two older brothers have helped pay for their education.

"All three boys have changed their major," said Buck's mom. "I might not have been thrilled about the fact. One was from graphic arts to psychology," she said, emphasizing the vast difference between the two majors and surprise at her son's profound change in direction. But she and her husband supported all of their sons' choices with some very practical and compassionate parenting. "My husband and I looked at each other. I'm not the one who is working their job for them. I wasn't the one going to college. What we insisted they do is have good communication with their advisor. They had to have a good plan and they did. '*You've* got to map it out,' and they did. It really wasn't for us to decide. It was going to cost more money. They have to contribute toward the cost of education. At some point you have to encourage them to do some of this themselves."

Of course not everyone is on the same page as this family. More than three-quarters of the students surveyed say they ask their parents for academic advice, most of them somewhere from weekly to monthly; 3 percent claim to do so even more frequently. For personal advice the frequency is even greater, with nearly 25 percent seeking advice somewhere between daily and weekly. Clearly it's a lot easier to speed-dial mom and dad than to make an appointment with a dean or advisor. But at least as far as academics go, a dean or advisor is probably the best source for relevant information.

### Relationships with Parents: Best Friends Forever?
Closeness between parents and children does have its advantages. The survey students say their relationships with mom and dad are generally strong, averaging 7.8 on a scale of 1 to 10. That's the good news. But there's some bad news here too: students whose parents do most of the dialing and emailing rated their parents as controlling and their relationships as fraught with conflict.

Rebecca, a senior at an elite liberal arts college, said during an interview that she gets up to eight emails a day from her mom, plus daily phone calls. Rebecca loves her mom, but struggles with that closeness. She's also had a tough time separating and making decisions on her own—hallmarks of adulthood. "I have to always check in," says Rebecca. "I always want her to validate my actions." This is a poignant commentary by someone who in an earlier era might have made that transition well before her last year in college.

On the other end of the spectrum, students who decide when to call home reported more positive feelings toward their mom and dad. Those with more balanced contact were more likely to see their parents as people they enjoy and want to be with. When students were more likely to initiate the calls, these warm feelings were stronger.

Abby's interviews with students and their parents at other colleges revealed a pattern similar to the survey data. A student at a Massachusetts college, Rick enjoys his parents, talking to and texting them a couple of times a week, about the Red Sox, classes, and internships. If the better part of a week goes by and his parents haven't heard from him, his mom usually calls, but by and large he initiates most contact, and his parents have let him set the tone throughout his three years in college. "Everyone is pretty laid back," he said. His mom remembered calling him early in his freshman year, probably a little too much; she heard the annoyance in his voice and backed off. Rick's dad also has been thoughtful about how he communicates. His respect for his son's growing independence is evident as he describes how Rick managed to secure a very competitive internship for the summer between junior and senior year, without anyone pulling strings for him. Through his internship connections Rick was able to snag a pair of coveted Red Sox tickets. "He took me to the game and was very proud of that," said his dad, sharing in his son's pride.

In fact Rick's relationship with his parents is so satisfying that he's surprised when his friends don't have such a bond with their parents, and he feels sorry for them. During freshman year he spoke in disbelief about classmates who regarded talking to their parents as "a chore and how much they hated it." He asked, "Am I lame that I like talking to my parents?" During junior year he talked about a friend at home who was miserable at college but couldn't tell her parents. "She said, 'It will just disappoint my dad a lot.' It's so foreign to me. Her parents are so controlling."

Rick likes his relationship with his parents. He has called the shots about how much he talks to them, does much of the initiating, feels good about both the amount and the quality of communication, and exhibits signs of independence. There are other students, however, who report strong relationships but who seem to be trading off independence for closeness, enmeshed in too frequent contact. Consider the student who shares her daily life with her "best friend," mom. This constant connection, where each choice and event in her life is discussed, creates an emotional bond that allows her little freedom to navigate on her own. Several students reported that Skype can intensify this bond in ways that keep them emotionally tethered to home. This is beyond what they expect or want during this time of life. One described with some anguish how her mother calls every day while making dinner, placing the laptop on the floor while they chat. That way the computer video camera captures the family dog as he walks back and forth, wagging his tale at the sound of her voice. Overall we found that students who were in the most frequent contact with mom and dad were less autonomous than those not in such frequent contact. These daily calls, check-ins, requests for advice, and help with problem solving may feel good to some parents and kids, but many parents might not feel the same if they knew it was keeping their kid from growing up. As in most things in life, the message here is *moderation*. Spacing the calls allows for a student to develop an independent life and create healthy emotional distance from home.

### Self-regulation: The Path to Academic Success

Another key to becoming independent is learning to successfully manage one's behavior, and for college students especially, learning how to manage their studies. This includes time management, organization, and a host of study skills. Students without these skills can

45

have a rough passage in college, especially with the relative lack of structure compared to high school years. Imagine students who have been told when, where, and how to study now trying to cope with the unbridled freedom of college.

In our surveys we gauged how students regulated their own academic work, asking them to respond to such statements as *I plan ahead for academic assignments* and *I set small goals for myself so I can keep up with bigger tasks.* Students who responded positively had good self-regulation. They also showed an enthusiasm for learning and satisfaction with both their academics and their overall college experience. *They had higher GPAs.* Not surprisingly they were also far less likely to procrastinate on papers and assignments than students who lacked these self-regulation skills. Interestingly, the same students also reported satisfying relationships with their parents and showed a high degree of autonomy.

Clearly becoming a self-regulated learner is an important part of a positive college experience. Parents who gradually ease up on supervising their child's studies during high school will help her become a happier and more capable student in college. This doesn't happen overnight; it's a carefully orchestrated process of letting up a bit at a time, relaxing the monitoring and letting the adolescent take ownership of her learning. By the time college applications roll around, the results will be evident in the child who initiates the process, doesn't expect her parents to complete the forms, and knows that it's not "we" who are applying to college.

*Parental Regulation*

There is simply no doubt that self-regulation is good and that parents and universities should help foster these skills. Unfortunately, some parents are still regulating their college-age child's academic behaviors. We asked participants to agree or disagree with statements such as *My parents edit the papers I write* and *My parents check with me to make sure I'm keeping up with homework.* The parents whose kids responded positively may have had the best intentions of helping, but these practices were counterproductive. In fact, as our data show, they went hand-in-hand with frequency of communication with parents and also with procrastination, not a habit that parents want to strengthen. Parents who call the most often are using these calls to micromanage their child's academic life and may be robbing him of the motivation to do the work independently.

Parents who think they are being helpful by calling often and giving reminders or actually helping their child do his work need to know that they might not be helping him at all, either psychologically or academically. In fact our research shows that the more parents tried to help academically, the less autonomous and less independent students perceived themselves to be. Not surprisingly these students also portrayed themselves as inept at managing their coursework. Maybe parents are trying hard to help the least independent, most procrastinating kids, but *it doesn't seem to be working.*

It would be better for parents to help their kids become self-regulated, teaching them in high school how to manage their time, take notes, study for tests, or helping them find out where to do this in college. Parents can refer student to study skills centers, for example. Students also reported that they like being nagged in college even less than they did in high school. Small wonder that their academic motivation flags as a result. For example, Seth, a sophomore, began to submit papers later and later, struggling to find the energy for work that no longer felt like his own, as his grades dropped. His parents' constant oversight had depleted his enthusiasm for learning. He ended up seeking help for a problem that by that point was far greater than procrastination, as he was falling further and further behind and caring less all the time.

One of the most disturbing findings in our studies is that students reported that parents are proofreading (19 percent) and editing (14 percent) their college papers. Students have many authorized opportunities to get this kind of help, typically from those trained in how to develop writing skills. Parents who work on their kids' papers may keep them from the type of learning colleges promote. And they may very well be embarrassing themselves and their kids. We heard from several professors who routinely ask to have papers submitted electronically and who were stunned and disgusted to see the use of the "track changes" software feature, with a parent's comments and corrections in the margins. When this happens most faculty members we talked with call the student in for discussion and explain that they expect the work to be the student's own. The discovery of these behaviors may still be new and startling to many faculty members; typically there is no way to know just how many students have had parental help but covered their tracks, and most papers are not submitted electronically. Institutional guidance seems to be lacking at this point, again because the extent of this problem wasn't known until now. What's needed are more preventive measures, including warning students in advance about what kind of help is appropriate and fair and what is not, and making sure that parents get this message as well.

Some parents are also continuing to regulate behavior apart from academic life, reminding the emerging adult, just as they might have reminded the adolescent at home, about what to eat and how much to sleep. We asked students to tell us how often their parents called with such reminders. The more often parents called their kids, the more likely they were to make such reminders. Not surprisingly parents who called about these details of daily life also prodded their kids about academic issues.

Students who reported a high frequency of these reminders from parents were also less autonomous in multiple ways. They were less independent, were less likely to see their parents as people apart from their role as parents, and had lower scores on emotional autonomy.

They also showed less skill at managing their studies and time, had lower GPAs, and had less satisfaction with their college experience and learning. Their relationship with their parents was more likely to be characterized by conflict and control issues.

Once upon a time, struggling students might have gone to college and tried to figure it out on their own or gotten help from resident assistants, deans, counseling staff, peer tutors, faculty advisors, and writing centers. It seems to make more sense to steer students toward these services and teach them to seek help when they need it.

Students whose parents intervene so frequently have little reason to develop either self-regulation or appropriate help-seeking skills. Lacking these skills will hinder them in college and later in adult life, in relationships, and in the work world. College is a time for taking charge of academic responsibilities and for learning how to learn. Parents who intervene inappropriately are blocking this process.

## Parental Involvement: Dialing It Back During College

Knowing when to intervene (and there are some appropriate instances that we discuss later) can be a struggle for parents, especially after all the years of being told to get involved. Schools urge parental engagement from the early years, hosting open houses and parent-teacher conferences, scheduling parent helpers in the classroom, conferring with parents about how to help with homework, and pushing for parental involvement in class projects and other assignments. Although this works well in earlier years, little is known about its value in the college years. (Perhaps there has been no reason to research a practice that wasn't expected to continue when kids left home.) Parents who have continued their involvement right up through the marathon of college admissions may not know when, how, or why to back off. It worked to get their kid into a good school, so they see no reason to stop now.

49

For some students the move to college is easier because in high school their parents encouraged them to make their own decisions and become less dependent. Harris, now a sophomore at New York University, had some challenges adjusting during his first year, but they were not unexpected. With undergrads numbering about twenty-one thousand and its Greenwich Village campus, NYU was a huge change from his much smaller, suburban high school, and it took a while for Harris, an intense and somewhat reserved student, to find his way around and to join a community of friends. The fact that he tried very hard and unsuccessfully to keep a relationship going with a girlfriend still in high school back home (something he'll never regret, he said) did slow his transition. Overall, though, Harris didn't have much trouble with the decision end of things at college. "It was a new freedom," he said. "But my parents were not that restrictive with me in high school. They gave me a lot of freedom." Worried about how that might sound, he added quickly, "They really cared a lot about me." Harris is close to his parents, speaking to them a couple of times a week; he and his parents initiate the contact equally. Harris also has had little trouble keeping up with his course work at the very competitive NYU, maintaining close to an A average. "My parents aren't really involved in my classes," he said. Since being at college he's "gotten a lot closer" to his parents. They have developed some common interests, and skirmishes revolving around life at home ("Clean up your room!") have evaporated. "Those small things cause the most tension," Harris said.

## Advice for Parents

As students go through college parents may want to help them make the most of it by keeping in mind both short- and long-term outcomes. They can do that by helping their children take charge of their own lives so that they are less in need of parental support on a daily basis.

Students also need to know more about their own development and how to approach college with an eye toward long-term goals. It's too easy to send a paper home with an urgent plea. ("Help! My paper is due in the morning and I need you to proof it for me!"). Parents aren't the only culprits in calling too much. Both parties can reexamine their behavior and think about where it leads. Reading and discussing this chapter might be a helpful place to begin.

If your children are still in high school, now is a good time to encourage them to take more responsibility for their lives, and for you to take less. This is particularly important if you still coordinate their schedules and remind them of school tasks. Teach your children to use an academic planner; you can introduce the idea by saying that it's a skill needed in college. Tell them you believe they are old enough to remember when practices are scheduled and assignments are due. Similarly if you have fallen into the habit of perpetually reminding your children about homework or studying for tests or starting papers, try shifting that responsibility. You can say, "I know I've done a lot in the past to remind you of what you need to do. But I know you are old enough now to take responsibility for yourself and accept the consequences. I am always available to help you, of course."

We encourage parents to think back to their own college years or the time they first left home. It can be helpful to consider how often you talked to your parents then, what you talked about, and where you went for advice when you had a problem with a roommate or difficulty in a class. How much say did your parents have in your choice of major, and how much help did they give you academically? Just because technology makes it possible to stay so involved doesn't make it necessary or advisable, and too frequent communication may make it too easy to offer advice more than is actually helpful.

Knowing the dangers of too much of the wrong kind of communication can help both parents and their college-age kids. How parents communicate is as important as what they say and affects whether their kids feel controlled or supported. Keeping an eye on the big picture and larger goals—a healthy, independent, emerging adult who is well connected to his or her parents—can prevent rushing in to help when it's not in the best interest of the child.

## Chapter 4

# What Colleges and Universities Say When iConnecting Crosses the Line

For generations a college romance has been a rite of passage. Some students fall in love and their relationship lasts, but for others it's over in a blink, with one initiating the breakup and the other left to work through his or her misery with friends on campus. But now, as we found in exploring the iConnected parenting trend, kids often call parents first when trouble looms, and that includes messy breakups on campus. At home, work, and on the road, parents hear their child sob about being dumped. Depending on the child, these calls can go on for quite a while, rising in emotional pitch and increasing in number.

That's what happened recently when a couple broke up during their first year of college and the young woman didn't want the relationship to end. She blanketed her parents, especially her mom, in a blizzard of unhappy messages and calls. Her concerned parents responded, her mom flying out twice to see her. What happened next is over the top, at least in the college's eyes. As the breakup got messier (the guy wanted to just "be friends," but the girl couldn't tolerate that), both students' parents asked the college to intervene and help the unhappy ex-couple sort through their relationship, as it was.

That request amazed college officials.

"It was the first time in thirty years that I had to mediate a relationship on that level," said the administrator who recounted the episode and asked not to use his school's name for fear of revealing the students' identities. "We're talking about a run-of-the-mill relationship here," he said in exasperation. "The thing to me is the level of involvement that the parents are playing in what should be an experience for these two kids to figure out how to walk through life. The kids aren't calling the shots," he said in disbelief. "How many breakups did I have in college? Six," he said, adding that he never would have involved his parents in them, let alone school officials!

While several factors (including the parents' misguided perception of the college's role) brought the breakup to his unwilling attention, the educator singled out one in particular: the parents' and kids' ability to communicate 24/7. Each upsetting message and call pulled the parents deeper into their daughter's drama: "She constantly updates them about her life, whether texting, emailing, or calling. Even though they are a thousand miles away, they are in constant contact with her life." The parents also used technology to drag college officials into the scenario. "They are emailing me constantly to try to help micromanage the situation." (The situation finally got resolved when one of the pair went abroad to study.)

Most parents hate to see their child unhappy, and when a continual stream of messages magnifies a kid's distress parents can get carried away. While this incident shouts *helicopter,* it is part of what's happening on campuses across the country. Bound by close relationships and good intentions, parents cross the line of appropriate behavior every day as they try to insulate their kids from predictable woes: an imperfect paper, being late for class, an inconsiderate roommate, even a broken heart. In many of these cases, ease of communication aids and abets parents in their efforts.

In the pages ahead we show the most common blunders that well-meaning parents make. More important, we also show how the college community views the families involved in these missteps and the consequences of their actions. But first, in order to better understand the colleges' perspective, let's walk through a little recent history on parents and the college scene.

## Colleges and Parents: A Changing, Challenging Relationship

Colleges' attitudes toward parents have shifted in recent years. Initially, as the helicopter hype began to peak, many colleges resisted parents' efforts to become more involved on campus. Of course administrators have long been happy to see families support their children's schools—donations are always welcome!—but they've been less inclined to accept parents' participation in their children's lives on campus. As involved parenting became a part of life and the cost of college continued to rise, however, some schools began making more space for parents.

Meanwhile the Internet has given parents the ability to track down college administrators more efficiently than in the past. And the round-the-clock access that cell phones and email provide has spawned a vast new stream of communication between college officials and concerned parents. Even at schools like Pitzer College in California, a college known for attracting independent-minded students, administrators find themselves awash in messages from involved parents. "Some of our parents, I swear they want to be at Pitzer more than their kids do," jokes Jim Marchant, Pitzer's dean of students and vice president of student affairs. This more intense communication is a challenge for many schools, and across the board administrators are thinking more strategically about how to interact with parents.

Many schools do make a point of telling parents to give their kids space. In letters, emails, and often gently humorous talks at orientations for families of first-year students parents are urged to just let go. But it's hard to tell how effective these efforts really are. Parent pages on college websites are now becoming de rigueur and parent associations on campus are growing steadily, according to Marjorie Savage and Katherine Wartman, authors of the book *Parental Involvement in Higher Education: Understanding the Relationship among Students, Parents and the Institution.* Many colleges have become more receptive to the participation of students' families on campus, but underneath much of the administrations' talk about parents as partners lies unease shared by a sizable group of educators. Some are concerned by aggressive parents demanding a larger role in their kids' college lives. While they may pay lip service to the concept of engaging the whole family, many educators just want to focus on what they know best, educating students, not managing their parents. Indeed, one college administrator wearily told us he wanted to name the school's new parent website "It's Not about You!" Parents may want to keep this thought in mind before dialing or emailing their child's professor, residence advisor, or dean of students.

## Mistakes Parents Make When Dealing with Their Children's Colleges

### Calling Too Much

Many college educators worry when they see students and parents in constant touch. As we noted earlier, we fear such behavior undercuts students' ability to create solid friendships and other sources of support on campus. Some experts believe that it also prevents or delays freshmen from feeling that they really belong at their new school. "Parents and family members are the biggest violators now that there are so many electronic tethers," said Houston Dougharty, vice president for student affairs at Grinnell College "They say, 'If I'm just emailing or calling a couple of times per day, it's not the same as interfering in their lives.' Well, in fact, it is." It bothers Dougharty when students whip out their cell phones as soon as they leave class, seemingly unaware of the students walking next to them. "There's a real loss because they are not putting the effort into the relationships that are right beside them physically. It's poignant for us at Grinnell. People come to school here because of the tight-knit community." Of course students may be talking to friends on campus or at other schools, but chances are that a good number are talking to mom and dad. Parents would be wise to think twice about calling too much, especially during a student's first semester, when fitting in and making new friends is crucial. We understand that some kids may encourage their parents' calls, and parents respond because, after all, they can't see for themselves what's really going on there.

## Accepting Only One Side of the Story

One troubling aspect of all this contact between parents and kids is that parents are getting only their child's side of the story. Part of this stems from technology (we hear only what the caller tells us), but sometimes children resort to this selective narrative when there's trouble afoot. College students may report their version of events ("I got a C on that test! The professor didn't even tell us what to study!"), sometimes omitting unfavorable and vital details ("I skipped class last week"). Although this was also true in past generations, today's immediacy of communications may encourage more of this kind of omission. Now students call in the passion of the moment, wanting to tell their side of the story, and to find someone to please say they are right!

Some students are unwilling to accept responsibility for whatever fix they find themselves in. (They are not likely to say "Hmmm, maybe I shouldn't have drunk that second six-pack of beer" or "I probably shouldn't have copied those sections from my roommate's old term paper.") "Sometimes what happens in that visceral moment of response when students have been told they are in trouble, a human response is to lash back and to say, 'No, I didn't do it,'" said James Terhune, dean of students and vice president of student affairs at Colby College, a small liberal arts college in Maine, who has seen this scenario multiple times.

When backed against the wall, many students call their parents. "I've had the experience in my office of students who don't like what I'm saying to them speed-dial mom and dad in the middle of the conversation," said Terhune. "What used to happen, when there was more lag time, you had to sit down and actually type or write a letter to your parents about what happened. You might think twice before you folded it up, put it in an envelope with a stamp, and mailed it. Email happens instantly. Now when they've started down a particular path [with their version of events] they can't turn back, and it becomes that much more difficult." Sometimes, in the rush for validation, students become stuck with their false version of events, and some eventually believe it to be true.

That factor played a big role in the nasty breakup described earlier. As it turned out, the young woman failed to tell her parents that she sometimes yelled at her ex when she ran into him on campus.

### Assuming Your Child's Role

For many parents, figuring out how much to be involved in their children's campus lives isn't easy. From preschool through high school parents are so conditioned to help their children that, when it's time for college, they aren't sure what to do. Jim Terhune, who is also a dad of teenagers, empathizes with today's parents. "The line that we all keep looking to define is at what point does that parent's involvement cross from being mentor, parent, guidance counselor, or coach into acting as a surrogate for a son or daughter," he said. For many parents that line is hard to see, and having a round-the-clock connection to their kids makes it even harder.

With cell phones and video chats, parents now experience their children's lives on a real-time basis, much like in *24,* the adrenaline-pumping television hit that each week details one hour in the life of an antiterrorist agent. The immediacy (and, sometimes, the emotion) tempts parents—even those who know better—to jump in and solve their children's problems. Patricia M. Lampkin is vice president and chief student affairs officer at the University of Virginia. She's also a mom of two college-age children, and this is how she describes her reaction when they call with problems: "I have to literally hold myself back on not giving the answer or my opinion."

What makes it even tougher is that many students aren't afraid to ask their parents to step in when things don't go their way. Our surveys show that one out of twelve students admits to asking his parents to call a dean or a professor to get a grade changed or finagle a new housing arrangement. (Because these data are reported by the students themselves, we think such calls for help may happen even more often than that.)

Frequently students who are caught in the emotion of a moment call their parents to complain. They don't explicitly ask their parents to jump in to fix things, but some moms and dads inevitably do (and later may wish they hadn't). Typically college officials circle back to the student, who then says, according to one college president, "My mother told you WHAT??? I was just calling to vent!" Even some of these protests, however, should be taken with a grain of salt, as some students know just how their parents will react when their distress call comes in. When put on the spot, well after the heat of the moment, the students may be embarrassed at the trouble they caused.

*Fighting Your Child's Battles*

Without having the benefit of the full story, and because of the immediacy of our 24/7 communications cycle, some parents charge off on behalf of their children. Parents may feel compelled to act when their child calls in tears or anger about a wrong or a slight from another student, often a roommate or other students living on their floor. In some cases, parents have even decided to call the roommate themselves. "The mother will call the child's roommate and say, 'Why are you being mean to my daughter? How come you went to Applebee's and didn't take my daughter?'" said Sarah English, director of housing and residential life at Marist College in New York. Some students even welcome their parents' interventions. "The apple doesn't fall far from the tree," English said, meaning that if parents don't respect the traditional boundary around a situation in which they should not intervene, the child may share the same attitude.

English and other college officials believe that such calls are a bad idea: "[Parents] cross the line when they are calling the roommate." Parents are adults, and it's unfair and inappropriate to wield their parental weight against a student.

Other parents take a less direct route, reaching out instead to the offending students' parents. One mother, Susan, whose daughter attended a prominent southern university, was shocked when Jane, the mother of her daughter's roommate, called and asked, "Have you heard what's going on between the girls?" Of course, Susan had, but she didn't let on. As it turned out, Susan's daughter wanted to room with someone else for the fall semester because her roommate was too controlling about what to put on the walls, when to turn out the lights, and other details of dorm life. Jane was calling to make the case for the two students to continue rooming together and to blackball the new roommate. Although Jane didn't actually come straight out and ask Susan to intervene with her daughter, the subtext was unmistakable. "The conversation was very civilized. But I was very clear that I wasn't going to get involved," said the surprised Susan. "Today, they fight. Tomorrow, they're best friends. I feel it is part of growing up, spreading their wings."

Roommate problems have to be extreme for housing officials to step in. The general philosophy is that students need to adjust to each other's differences and that learning to do so is an essential part of growing up and a vital life skill. If students can't come to an agreement, they can always appeal to their school's residence life people, who are trained to handle these situations. If things are really bad between roommates, however, school officials will take action.

Most schools expect students to contact housing officials about faulty air conditioners, burned-out lightbulbs, and dripping shower heads. Doing so builds responsibility and independence. Parents who continually hound residence life staff about a torn window screen or a new drawer for their child's bureau may find they get a slower response to their minor complaints than parents calling infrequently about similar problems. As the old saw goes, the squeaky wheel gets the grease, but in residential life circles sometimes the quiet wheel gets the grease more quickly when it does squeak. That's another good reason why parents would do well to encourage their students to take charge themselves of their roommate concerns and other housing issues.

### Posing As Your Child Online

With so much college business conducted online, it's a snap for parents to do what their children should be doing. Again and again college administrators have told us about parents who obtain their child's college password and use it to gain access to their school email and interact with the college, just as if they were the student.

In some instances the results are not exactly what the parents or their children were hoping for. One mother of a first-year student at Davidson College in North Carolina tried to log on to the school's registration website to register her child for classes (something students normally do for themselves). Her first few attempts failed, recalled a Davidson official. The mom might have waited a reasonable period of time and then tried again, but she didn't. She plowed ahead, attempting to log on seventy-five times in thirty minutes. Her persistence didn't pay off as she had envisioned; instead she managed to crash the entire registration website. Her child was mortified, and college officials and other students were frustrated. The student "came in and was so embarrassed," said Leslie Marsicano, Davidson's assistant dean for academic administration.

Colleges discourage students from sharing their passwords with anyone, including parents. We recognize that parents may have become accustomed to monitoring their child's online activities during earlier years for reasons of safety, but if this control hasn't yet been surrendered, now is the time. Managing college correspondence, registration, and other online academic interactions is part of learning how to accept responsibility and govern one's own behavior, and students need to do these tasks themselves. When mom and dad are accessing their children's registration systems and email, they are interfering with the kids' ability to become independent and to separate from home. Parental involvement on this level also makes it easy for mom and dad to intervene academically—which is also inappropriate.

## Collaborating and Cheating

Just as they did during their kids' high school years, some parents continue to proofread and help write their kids' college papers via email. Our research revealed that one out of five students at Middlebury and Michigan admits to emailing papers home to parents before turning them in to professors. But these schools' students are far from alone in this practice. Interviews with students and faculty in a diverse sample of colleges and universities show that this practice occurs just about everywhere. Honor codes have been slow to adapt to what happens in many students' homes before and after they come to college. Dr. Walter Rankin, associate dean for academic affairs at the School of Continuing Studies at Georgetown University, explains in an email, "We [faculty and administrators] tend to think of honor codes as unchanging, historically ethical guidelines that anyone would understand, but as we have seen, the level of parental involvement has grown exponentially in recent years to the point that we in higher education often have a very different understanding of what's 'original' work in comparison to what our students have learned at home." Rankin chairs the school's Honor Council and has worked on the administration of honor codes for more than ten years and presented papers on the topic at the American College Personnel Association and the National Academic Advising Association. "We have operated largely on a false assumption that our students would simply not send their papers home to their parents for editing and revising because the parents themselves would know this is not ethical or allowable," he said. Dr. Andrew Van Schaack, a professor at Vanderbilt University, found in one course that 41 percent of his students (mostly sophomores) admitted to having parents help with their assignments; about 90 percent said they knew someone who did.

Not so very long ago students couldn't zip a paper home for parents to edit; snail mail was too cumbersome, and culturally it just wasn't cool for parents to be so engaged in a college student's life. But today this kind of academic intervention is the norm for many families. Increasingly parents are calling faculty members with detailed questions about assignments and papers. Some even call to argue about a grade on a paper, compelled in part because *they* worked on it.

"I have spoken firsthand to a parent who said, 'I know his paper was right because I edited it,'" reported Dr. Teresa Fishman. The incident occurred when she was teaching at Purdue University, after a student complained to her about the low grade she'd received on a paper. When Fishman refused to change the grade the parent called. "I was very surprised that they would say that they had worked on their student's paper—as if there was nothing wrong with that." What Fishman remembers most clearly is her shock at the parent's admission, and feeling constrained by FERPA, the Family Educational Rights and Privacy Act, from talking about the impact of the parent's actions on the student's grade. FERPA gives parents access to their children's school records in the earlier years, and then transfers those rights to the students when they turn 18 or enter a postsecondary institution at any age. Under FERPA, colleges may grant parents access to their children's records with the students' consent. Additionally, colleges may, but aren't required to, grant access if the student is a confirmed tax dependent. At the time, Fishman was unaware of the student's status in respect to their FERPA rights. "I couldn't say 'You are messing up your student by doing their work.' But I'm pretty sure I told them it wasn't a good idea to work on their child's assignments." In any case she didn't change the student's low grade. Fishman is now a professor and director of the Center for Academic Integrity, a nonprofit organization based at Clemson University that works to promote academic honesty in higher education.

Most educators are unhappy about this new crop of "unauthorized collaborators," who are violating the principles of academic integrity as well as interfering with their children's ability to learn and do for themselves. At Middlebury and other schools students sign a pledge on each assignment and test, stating that they have not received any unauthorized aid. At institutions with such honor codes, help from an instructor, teaching assistant, or college writing center is typically allowed. In some instances professors may allow students to work with their classmates on group projects or other assignments. No institution, to our knowledge, has yet included parents in this list of "authorized aid," but few have thought to formally exclude them either, as this problem just hasn't been on their radar until recently. Some students and their parents interpret this as license for mom and dad to step in.

Part of what might be driving parental overinvolvement in their children's academic work is that today's parents are better educated than those of generations past. Parents with children in college today are far more likely to have a college degree than parents of college students in the mid-1970s, according to the National Center for Education Statistics. This under-the-radar help also furthers inequity in education; faculty members are unlikely to know which papers got parental help and which didn't (unless students forgot to remove their parents' edits). Not all students have access to these resources. The first-generation college students may suffer in the grading process as they struggle to learn the skills that others aren't pressed to develop.

One student at George Mason University in Fairfax, Virginia, wrote a paper that the professor determined he had plagiarized, but the student said it wasn't his fault. It was his mom's. "The son said that she had in fact plagiarized the paper. The mother was in fact doing it and the son was accepting it. That was horrible," said Walter Rankin, who heard the case at George Mason while serving as a deputy associate dean for academic affairs.

Some parents feel pressure to help their kids simply because so many other parents are doing the same. Teresa Fishman herself has two college-age children who would love to have her help out on assignments like other parents do. "They say, 'Why can't you be like the other parents?' Now we've had to have really serious talks about what I can do and can't do. For example, 'I can give comments and suggestions, but I can't do anything on your paper.'"

Students have told us that they consider getting help from their parents to be the same as going to the writing center. But the difference is that, at the centers, instructors and sometimes students' peers suggest ways to improve their papers; they teach them rules and techniques for better writing, but they won't help rewrite the students' work. "The writing center won't take an email at ten p.m. before the paper is due and make edits on your work, and your mom and dad might," said Andrew Van Schaack of Vanderbilt.

While some parents may check their students' papers for typos, others actually make substantial edits, rephrasing sentences, rearranging paragraphs, and adding new concepts and information. That kind of editing amounts to cheating. "It's like buying a paper from someone. It's plagiarism. It's inappropriate," said Dr. Louise Douce, a psychologist and assistant vice president for student life and director of the Counseling and Consultation Service at Ohio State University.

Some students also view this practice as dishonest. At the very competitive University of Virginia students are immersed from day one in a culture of trust built on the school's rigorous honor code. A former chair of the university's Honor Committee puts it this way: "Students here are on a level playing field where they are writing their own papers, and that's part of the community of trust here: you can trust your next-door neighbor to turn in her own paper. So why would you one-up her?"

At the University of Minnesota one senior, the first in his African-American family to attend college, expressed a different take on the trend: "My mom didn't go to college and she asks *me* to read over the letters that *she* writes because she's nervous that she won't have used the right word." Asked what he thought about students who did send their papers home for help from their parents, he said, "I almost feel like it is a form of cheating. Do your work yourself!"

Moral issues aside, educators also tend to oppose parental help because students aren't really learning how to write, and that can have unfortunate consequences in the long run. Students who don't know how to write well are going to enter the workforce with a false sense of abilities. "They get back papers that have A's and they forget that mom and dad went through and cleaned up spelling and grammar and maybe clarified some ideas in their paper," said Van Schaack. "Clarity of communication is a skill. Just having a good idea is not enough. Being able to really communicate that idea is oftentimes the difference between a successful [and an unsuccessful] attorney or a writer or a scientist. That's what I'm trying to train them on."

While colleges have been slow to recognize this trend, as it is not easy to identify, some schools are beginning to develop strategies, such as giving more assignments that have to be written in class or that depend largely on content addressed only in class. A few professors are even considering declaring in their course syllabi that such parental help is forbidden. Colleges are certain to be less forgiving of students and parents who they find participating in this kind of behind-the-scenes collaboration. Although the Center for Academic Integrity has yet to adopt an official stance on this issue, Teresa Fishman, its executive director, believes that the solution lies in educating the parents. "The parents misunderstand the goal of the assignment. It is not to develop a great paper but to develop a great student," she said. "We've become so object-oriented that there's such a tremendous weight attached to all these assessments. The assessment isn't the goal; it's actually an indicator of how the student is doing. There's a disconnect between the goal of the teacher and what the parent sees as the immediate goal." This disconnect often leads to tension between parents and faculty, especially when mom and dad try to contact their child's professor themselves.

*Hunting Faculty*
There's a wealth of information about college curricula and faculty contact information on college websites and other Internet sources. That ease of access plus the reality of how much families are paying

for their kid's college education create a lot of chances for parents to overstep.

"Parents can have this direct access to faculty members that they didn't have before, that didn't happen ten or twelve years ago. Everyone is so savvy about tracking people. It even starts in the summer," said Jane Martindell, dean for academic advising and support at Kenyon College in Ohio. One of Barbara's colleagues received a voicemail in July from a parent who asked that she fax her fall syllabus to his office so that his daughter could get a head start on the reading for the course. She replied that she hadn't completed the syllabus and would be handing it out to everyone the day classes began.

For some parents the temptation to talk directly to their children's professors is irresistible. Some want to make sure their child gets enrolled in the right courses; others want to make excuses for missed classes or plead for extensions on their child's papers or take-home exam; still others call to discuss or contest their child's grades.

As parents have become more involved on campus the volume of calls has grown and faculty members are becoming more accustomed to hearing from mom and dad. But that doesn't mean they like it. "They see it as interfering," says Martindell. Professors would rather hear directly from students of course. Parents' overinvolvement also makes faculty members question students' ability to function in class, on campus, and in the world outside college. "They'll say, 'This poor kid, no wonder they struggle.' Sometimes it creates more sympathy for the kids, and sometimes it creates negative feelings," says Martindell. Professors who question a student's judgment and independence are unlikely to give him a stellar reference for an internship or graduate school. It's unreasonable to expect professors to use up their professional chits on students who can't advocate for themselves. Parents would do well to encourage their kids to seek help on their own, including initiating conversations with faculty members.

### *Robbing Kids of the Ability to Make Decisions*

With the constant contact between parents and kids, educators worry about students' ability to make decisions on their own and what that bodes for the students' future.

Kirk Manning, vice president of student life and dean for student development at St. Thomas Aquinas College in New York, likes to tell the story of a young woman at Widener College, where he recently served as associate provost and dean of students. The student was talking on her cell phone in the dining hall, but otherwise immobilized. "I hear one end of the conversation. She says, 'They are having hamburgers today. Should I have a hamburger?'" As the lunch debate continued Manning realized that the girl was talking to her mother. "The point is that she can't even make a decision about what to have for lunch without talking to her mom."

Mark Reed, vice president of student affairs at Fairfield University in Connecticut, describes this phenomenon as a "paralysis of choice." He says two factors contribute to it. First, because students are so close to their parents, they may depend on them to help make decisions. The second cause stems from our technology. Students today are so connected to their cell phone, laptop, even their iPod that they have little time to just think on their own. Yet, as Reed points out, the ability to reflect independently is key to building decision-making skills. But the new dynamic of round-the-clock communication and involved parenting is changing that. From choosing their child's lunch to deciding what the child will major in, parents are involving themselves in the decision-making process more than ever. The results are not usually desirable.

Our studies have shown that parents are now weighing in heavily on their child's choice of major, which is not always what the child wants to study and not necessarily what's best for her. Martindell recently counseled a student nearing the end of her sophomore year who wanted to change her science major. Her father was a physician and had pressed her to go into the sciences. "It finally hit her that she doesn't really enjoy the science courses. It's a great realization to have. But she could have had it sooner." Changing majors nearly halfway through college may mean that the student has to take extra courses or take an additional year to graduate. It also means that the student spent nearly half of her very expensive education on studies that she didn't really like and eventually didn't pursue. This kind of mandated path for students is also dismaying to professors, who want students to be passionate, or at the very least interested, in the courses they teach.

Some level of parental involvement is understandable. The race to get into college emphasizes competitive transcripts. Even when a child is in college, families worry about academic records and how they'll appear to graduate schools or employers. Some parents fear that without their guiding hand their children will make mistakes and hurt their chances for law school or a career. This anxiety is familiar to many college administrators and faculty members, but it doesn't sit well with them to have parents communicating with them about their worries. Parents need to allow their children to learn from their mistakes. When parents worry overtly their angst is often absorbed by their kids, which makes the kids fearful of taking the kinds of risk that are appropriate in college: signing up for a challenging class or trying a different sport or a new activity that helps them become their own person.

During Kenyon's orientation sessions for new parents Martindell typically encourages parents to let their kids make decisions. Sometimes she meets resistance. "I've had parents say in information sessions, 'How can you be sure that my son won't make a huge mistake that will ruin his future?' And I said, 'I actually want your son to make a mistake.'" As we all know, we learn from our mistakes. College educators know this, and parents who overprotect their kids frustrate them as well as the college personnel who are there to help guide them.

Colgate University, a private college in upstate New York, has built a reputation for asking parents to stand back and let their kids resolve their own problems. "Overcoming a little discomfort, persevering through failure, and problem solving are key features of a Colgate education," said Beverly Low, Colgate's dean of first-year students. "One of the phrases that we use with parents is that we will not 'swoop in and fix things' because it robs [students] of an opportunity to learn. It's okay for students to struggle a little bit, to be challenged by a class or a roommate who is different from them."

For the most part college educators want to focus on teaching students. Parental blunders distract educators from their most important tasks and generate needless ill will for themselves and their children, even among the most compassionate college communities.

## Advice for Parents

Parents don't want their meddling to harm their children. While writing this book we often got asked how parents know when they've crossed the line, and we've come up with some basic tip-offs. If you find yourself becoming overly engaged in your child's love life or roommate disputes and other housing issues, you are close to the line, if not over it. The same goes for parents registering for their child's classes, gaining access to college email, picking majors, and contacting professors about assignments and grades. If you are editing your child's papers you are stepping well over the line and also may have violated ethical and academic honesty codes.

Parents who get caught up in the passion of their child's need of the moment and then rush in to fix things instead of giving him the support to sort out things himself are also entering questionable territory. When your child calls home with a crisis, listen carefully before responding. Find out what he's done to solve the problem. Help him consider the perspectives of others. Ask, "How do you think your roommate feels about this fight that you're having?"

On the whole, college administrators do appreciate parents who encourage their children to become independent and who respect what educators are trying to do: give students a good education and prepare them for life after college.

## Chapter 5

# Students' Concerns about Being So Close to Their Parents

When Sarah was assigned her first paper at her elite college, she asked her dad to edit it. He'd often done so before, revising papers and prepping her for tests, and even though Sarah was now at college he was still willing to help. With email it was so easy.

Like Sarah's dad, many parents have spent countless evenings at the kitchen table, proofreading their kids' high school papers for typos and bad grammar, even honing insights. The kids expect the help and are mostly grateful for it. Using email, some parents continue spending those nights editing college papers. In our research we found that one in five college students admitted sending papers to mom and dad before submitting them to their professors. While our reporting found some students to be up-front about this help from home, we also found others much less open about it (especially if their friends and other students frowned on the practice).

Teenagers who are close to adulthood may be open to support, but some feel uncomfortable about getting it. We talked to Sarah and other students in this chapter over a span of two years and learned how this emotional seesaw and constant contact with mom and dad shaped how they feel about themselves, their parents, and ultimately their college experience.

## Anxiety and Self-Doubt on Campus

Sarah felt frustrated after she emailed her first paper to her dad. "I can't even write a paper without getting my parents involved," she said, her voice low and halting as she recounted the episode. Sarah was sure that other students were writing papers without their parents' help. So many freshmen at her ultrahip college seemed accomplished and self-sufficient. What would they think if they knew she was getting help from her dad? It made Sarah feel different from her peers, just when she was trying so hard to fit in during those early days on campus. It also likely added to her stress. Nonetheless, despite her uneasiness, Sarah continued to email her papers home to her dad, and she continued to feel bad about it.

Sarah relied on her parents for more than just help with papers. Freshman year was tough for her. She didn't click with her roommate; she hung out, somewhat lost, in a big group of kids. She began calling her parents on her cell phone almost every day, spilling out the details of her new college life. And, of course, she emailed her papers to her dad. This was all so different from the independent life she had envisioned for herself in college, and it was hard for her to reconcile the two. Back when she was packing for college, her parents had asked how she wanted them to contact her. Email, Sarah replied, thinking it would keep her parents safely in the background until she had established herself there. She never dreamed that she would email and call so often.

Our research and reporting show that many college students share Sarah's conflict. They want and expect instant access to their parents, and they think they need it. (They also expect and want their parents' unconditional support, emotionally and practically.) At the same time some of these students have mixed feelings about being so close to mom and dad, especially when that relationship interferes with their independence or makes them feel inferior to more autonomous kids.

## Typical Ambivalence

Mixed feelings about parents are part of the teenage landscape, especially when kids are still living at home. In one breath your kids whisper they love you for helping them get ready for the prom; in the next they yell that they hate you for banning a coed sleepover afterward. It can be a frustrating, emotional time for everyone as children try to separate from their parents and still remain connected.

In college, many students find this 24/7 connection with parents comforting, but at times they find it irritating, even enraging. "I would be furious if my parents called every day," said Jim, a Middlebury senior who says he's close to his parents but remembers sometimes ignoring his mother's frequent calls freshman year. As parents try to manage their college kids' lives from afar, sometimes it's *what* parents say that annoys. ("Have you finished your Shakespeare paper yet?") In fact Barbara's research shows that nearly one-third of parents are still checking up on their children's college homework, not an advisable strategy at a time when young people very much need to take responsibility for their own learning. These behaviors can also undermine motivation. When schoolwork is constantly monitored by parents, kids wonder who they are really doing it for.

Traditionally conflict between parents and children lessened in college as kids moved away from home and their parents' watchful eye. But our research and reporting found that today, with cell phones and computers tethering kids and parents to each other, conflict can remain, and even get worse.

75

*Low Confidence and Trouble Adjusting*

Like Sarah, some college kids are embarrassed and confused by their heavy reliance on their parents. On some level they know that they are supposed to become more independent at college. They also feel pressure to enjoy college. How many times have they heard the refrain "These are the best four years of your life!" But for some students this is not the case at all.

Sarah is somewhat shy and was slow to settle into campus life. She is attending a college that is a big change from the high school she loved, which has clearly intensified her dependence and ambivalence. Sarah went to a small private school, where by design everybody made the team or got a part in the school play. It was a perfect fit for her. Her social life was simple, revolving around two close girlfriends. Her college is a far cry from that. It's bigger, more competitive, and less nurturing. Students are expected to be self-directed, capable, and very smart.

Aside from its academic excellence, her school is also known for its sophisticated student body. Sarah's demeanor and dress scream wholesome. During Abby's first interview with Sarah on campus, she wore simple corduroys and a fleece jacket. Soft-spoken, she blushed as she revealed her unanswered crush on an upperclassman.

Even after she became a sophomore Sarah was still secretly sending her papers home to dad, though not quite as much as she did the previous year. In one instance during freshman year she had procrastinated so long on a take-home exam that she didn't have time to get her dad's help and finished it only minutes before it was due. She assumed the paper was a disaster, but she got an A-. The episode did build her confidence, but not enough to keep her from seeking her dad's stamp of approval on her work.

She didn't use the campus writing centers because other students staff the centers and she didn't want them to judge her negatively. She equated her dad's help with going to the writing center, but without the judgment of her peers.

Sarah revealed that she continued to seek her dad's help because, as she said without a hint of irony, "Dad's a good confidence booster." Young children frequently seek their parents' approval for their new efforts. ("Mom, dad, watch me dive! Watch me swim! Watch me ride my bike!") But by the time kids reach college this need for parental approval should diminish. Yet Sarah constantly sought her parents' approval to validate her talents and decisions.

Sarah's parents, especially her dad, have always been powerful advocates for her—in some situations too much so. Sarah recalled an administrator at her high school urging her to speak for herself at a school conference rather than allowing her father to speak for her. When it came time to apply to colleges, her father was deeply involved in the entire process. With a backstory of such heavy parental involvement and her shy personality, Sarah sometimes struggled to find her own voice at college.

## Sarah's Senior Year

When Abby visited Sarah two years after her first interview, Sarah, now 21, was still in frequent contact with her parents but less torn about her dependence on them. In her junior year she was diagnosed with ADD (attention deficit disorder), a medical condition that makes it difficult for her to stay focused and organized. She said her parents had suspected as early as middle school that she had ADD. Recently she was also diagnosed with an anxiety disorder. Hearing these diagnoses gave Sarah a measure of comfort. "I have been concerned about being really dependent on my parents. That's something that I worried about a lot," she says. But now she understood why she has struggled academically and had come to rely so much on her parents. "[Learning that] has helped me feel like I'm not deficient," she said. Though she had made progress, including making some good friends and becoming active in campus activities, she noted, "I still depend on [my parents] a lot for advice and affirmation." Her feelings, especially in her early college years, reflect Barbara's findings that students whose parents still manage their academic lives lag behind their friends in becoming independent, separating from family and developing their study skills. This can be true for any student, including even those with a learning difference.

Looking back at her painful passage from high school to college Sarah allowed that she might have adapted more quickly if it hadn't been so easy to call her parents. Maybe things would have been better if she had hit it off with the students assigned to her floor freshman year. But she hadn't, and that added to her loneliness and stress. "When I get stressed out, I don't invest in friendships," she said. Even now that pattern continues to dog her. "When I get busy at school, I'm not great at maintaining relationships with friends. There are a lot of friends I haven't seen in a while. . . . [Instead] I will turn to my parents because it's easier." All it takes is a speed-dial home.

Given Sarah's personality, background, and attention and anxiety issues, she likely would have struggled in the early days at her competitive college. Yet her dad's continued and well-meaning help likely kept her struggling emotionally and academically. Without that help, Sarah might have gotten her issues addressed earlier and received the support and treatment she needed to manage them at college, getting help for her organizational and time management skills. She might have tried the campus writing center. If her papers hadn't been perfect, her professors would have given her feedback, helping her become a better writer. Instead Sarah's self-esteem seemed to have suffered during those years. As she herself has begun to realize, if she hadn't had her parents listening daily to all the details of her campus life in her first year, she might have tried harder to make new friends and share her experiences with them. Relying on her parents might have made her feel good for the moment, but it didn't address her anxiety, build her academic skills, or help her grow emotionally and socially, which, after all, is part of why she went to college.

Sarah's story is a cautionary tale for parents who want to help their kids a little too much, a little too often. Sometimes parents are so bent on helping their kids that they lose perspective. Wanting their kids to achieve socially and academically without struggle, parents end up crossing lines that they shouldn't, and even overlook important clues that indicate a learning difference or psychological issue. Overprotection can make children more vulnerable, awkward, and insecure than their peers.

## Regrets and Resignation

Even parents who do not help write their kids' college papers can become too involved in their children's campus life. Consider Shari, who was a sophomore when Abby first met her. A student at her state's large flagship university, Shari talked daily to her mom and dad. "They get mad when I don't call them," she said matter-of-factly. Even so, her parents did more of the dialing. She initially had her heart set on attending an out-of-state university but for financial reasons chose her state school. Enrolled in a very competitive preprofessional program, Shari studied hard despite some initial floundering with all the new free time . Her family didn't have much money, and she wanted a well-paying career. "My parents always joke that I'm going to get a big house in Florida with a little addition for them. My mom says she'll cook and clean for me. I don't know if they're serious, but I don't mind it."

Shari described her parents as "a little overprotective." During her freshman year she and her parents talked and emailed daily. They intervened in her roommate squabbles, which was easy to do because Shari and her roommate had been friends since they were 6 and the parents knew each other well. "Her parents are more protective than mine, if you can imagine that," Shari said with a knowing giggle.

79

Before each weekend in the fall of freshman year Shari's parents asked, "Are you coming home?" Their yearning to see her was implicit in the question. Shari initially resisted, wanting to dive into weekend life at college—and she did, attending lots of parties and making herself the designated caretaker of friends who got drunk.

One weekend, it was Shari's turn, and her account of that night reveals the pros and cons of this electronic bond between parent and child. At a party with her roommate, Shari got wasted. Without telling her roommate, she wandered back to her dorm and began suffering the inevitable consequences of having too much to drink. A decade ago this story probably would have ended here, but not today. Though much of the night was a haze, Shari was able to find her cell and call her hometown boyfriend. He alerted her parents, who then called her roommate at the party, insisting that she "go help Shari."

Early the next morning, Shari's parents arrived on the scene. She remembers her mother cleaning up the vomit that her roommate had missed. She also remembers how uncomfortable it was in her dorm room, now crowded with her disappointed parents and unhappy roommate. Her parents took her home for the rest of the weekend.

Later Shari's mom and dad called the roommate's parents about the incident. For the rest of the year the roommate's parents called constantly, trying without success to supervise *their* daughter from afar. (Shari ended up fielding their calls when her roommate rebelled, leaving her cell phone unanswered in their room.) Shari felt no remorse about what happened to her roommate, and she wasn't embarrassed by her parents' response. "I'm just glad that my boyfriend called my parents," she said.

Of course if a child is at risk, parents need to get involved. Parents do need to be concerned when their child gets drunk and is at risk for all kinds of bad things: sexual assaults, accidents, alcohol poisoning, and other injuries. Parents need to have a serious talk with their kids about drinking before they go to college and teach them how to look out for their friends. For example, students should never leave a party alone, especially if they have been drinking. In those situations, students need to have a buddy system (along with a designated driver, of course, if a car is involved). For parents, having the cell phone numbers of your kid's friends is a smart idea, and it can pay off in an emergency. But what about afterwards? Did Shari's parents need to clean her room, take her home, and call her roommate's parents? Could Shari have recovered from her hangover without their help?

College administrators and professors are amazed at how much students tell their parents. Most adults who were in college at least a decade ago never would have told their parents they'd gotten drunk. Nowadays many students share the details of their daily dramas, and some parents react.

One mother, according to a Davidson administrator, asked college staff to stop students from gossiping about her daughter. Her request astonished Davidson officials. The daughter's lack of embarrassment came as a bigger shock. "That's the biggest change," says Leslie Marsicano, Davidson's assistant dean for academic administration and former director of residential life. "Students used to say, 'My mother overreacts.' We don't see much of that anymore. Their expectation is that their parents will be involved on that level."

Shari grew up with that expectation. Her parents always helped her fix things. In middle school they called the principal when they felt a teacher just didn't like their daughter. "The teacher started being nicer to me because the principal started watching," Shari said with obvious satisfaction. As she got older she found her parents' behavior "kind of annoying," especially in high school, as she felt the tugs of adolescent independence. "They were 'helicopter parents,'" she said. During her college years her parents continued their hovering, via cell phone and email.

Away at college Shari enjoyed some personal freedom, despite her parents' vigilance from afar. That space proved just enough to let her

81

step back and become more understanding of her parents' behavior. Pragmatic at heart, she knew that alienating her parents wouldn't help her meet her career goals and live in that dream home in Florida. As a sophomore she still went home every other weekend. Home was a relief from the grind of competing for a spot in her challenging program; she slept on clean sheets, and her father made her favorite chicken and pasta dishes. She talked without enthusiasm about how she might "just as well go home" because it made her parents and boyfriend happy.

Most parents may not hover like Shari's, but there's a lesson here for all moms and dads. Even though kids may not *seem* to be adversely affected by their parents' continual contact, on some level they may well be. In Shari's case, though she accepted her parents' behavior, she wasn't entirely happy. There was more than a hint of resignation in her comments, a sense that she was missing out on what college might have been and exhaustion with fighting the pressure to go home. Her parents' financial and emotional support was helping her. In return she was giving up some independence and a chance to fully experience college. Whatever inner turmoil she felt about her parents' hovering had now morphed into a mixture of wistfulness and clear-eyed realism.

### Shari's Senior Year

When Abby visited Shari again in her senior year, she found her, now 21, still working hard and participating more in campus life. Since her sophomore year she had carved out more space for herself, away from her parents. "They see I have a clear goal and am making smart decisions. I think they get that I'm able to make decisions on my own," she said. She had broken up with her hometown boyfriend and no longer went home as much as she had in previous years. "I didn't really want to," she says, recalling how her parents and boyfriend pressured her to come home. Nonetheless her parents continued to press her to come home on weekends: "They still do that!" But now

Shari insisted on staying on campus most weekends; it was easier to study there, and she had more of a social life now. Her parents had come to accept her weekends at school, and Shari was careful to keep some details of her social life from her parents. But even when she went home her parents often called the cell phones of her high school friends, trying to find her when she was out. "I'm used to it," she said, but she had drawn the line at providing the numbers of her new friends on campus. After the incident freshman year she had never gotten that drunk again. Her old roommate had left college and was now living at home with her parents. "She hates it," Shari said.

At school Shari is quick to respond to her parents' calls. If she is at a party she'll step outside to talk. "I'll say politely, 'I'm out with my friends. Can I call you later?'" Overall she remains in very close touch with her parents, who initiate much of the contact. Her dad sends a daily text and her mom emails and phones. Some calls reflect her parents' anxiety: "They call all the time and say, 'Did you hear about that girl who got into the car accident?'" or some other catastrophe involving a college student.

One day, while she was at her part-time job, even though she is not supposed to use a cell phone at work, her dad texted and her mom called twice. Shari had just spent some time at home with them, recovering from bronchitis, and they wanted to make sure she was okay. Her mom, more than her dad, seems to have trouble observing traditional boundaries between parents and their nearly adult children. For example, after Shari broke up with her boyfriend he began to text her again, which Shari didn't appreciate. She told her mom, who immediately called him to stop. Shari had no idea that her mom had acted on her behalf, only learning about it through her ex. "I didn't really mind," she said.

While Shari sees herself as approaching adulthood, her easy acceptance of her mom's call to her ex-boyfriend suggests she may have a ways to go. At 21 many young people would see the behavior of

Shari's mom as intrusive, undercutting a growing ability to manage relationships with others. But Shari didn't. Maybe this was because the call met Shari's pragmatic needs: the ex backed off. Meanwhile Shari has become ever more the realist. She has discarded her dreams of Florida, deciding to try to stay in state after graduation, near her parents. "It's good to stay close to family and friends," she says, noting how difficult it was for her parents when they first moved away from their families. Besides, she says quickly, with a job there will be no time for the beach anyway. "That's what vacations are for." Now she is applying to her state university's graduate school program. If she is accepted at the lower-cost state university she plans to live with her parents until she completes the program at age 25. She realizes that moving back home may marginalize whatever independence she has achieved and that she will also have to contend with the growing gap between her and her mother (who didn't attend college), which has been created by her college education. Nonetheless she has undergraduate loans to repay (she's not sure how much she owes because her parents still handle most of her finances), and in some ways it will be easier to live at home. Still, Shari admits: "It kind of sucks being at home in your twenties." It certainly makes sense for a moderate-income student to avoid incurring even more debt, but Shari doesn't know the details of her own financial status or how much it would cost to live on her own.

Moving back home, Shari is choosing the path of least resistance, and she is both conflicted and resigned about her choice. For a good part of her college years she traded off independence and experience to please her well-meaning but overinvolved parents and achieve her professional goals. Now she is planning to do the same for graduate school. The fact that Shari is fuzzy about her financial situation and willing to let her parents manage that part of her life is not that unusual. As parents continue to take responsibility for their children's lives through the college years, students have little opportunity or incentive to learn much about managing their money or supporting themselves. Students who are more knowledgeable about their finances during college are likely to make an easier transition to adulthood. Parents can help by providing information and teaching money management skills.

## Best Friends with Baggage

Another growing phenomenon that we have encountered throughout our research and reporting is the evolution of the parent as best friend. This concept was nearly unheard of a couple of decades ago, but as kids' lives have become busier and parents have shifted closer, it has gained a foothold. Now a best-friend parent is common and seen by many kids and parents as mostly positive. In a survey that Barbara did of Middlebury parents, they spoke happily about the friendship quality of their roles. "It's almost a new convention where parents [today] are less authoritarian and more of a friend. Our parents missed a lot," commented one parent.

The best-friend parent is often the kid's go-to person, making travel plans, identifying key contacts for internships, jobs, and academic projects, and jumping in whenever the child seems to need help. The kids are well aware of their parents' abilities to take care of business for them.

Molly, a slim, polished senior at a northeastern college, said of her mom, "In high school she was my backup notebook. She always knew when my appointments and lacrosse practices were. She literally was my best friend." And in college she remained so. Every day Molly and her mother talked by cell phone and, just as she always had, mom ran interference for her. "When I went to college I didn't quite notice the transition. She was still doing the behind-the-scenes work," Molly said. One day Molly called to say she was sick, not terribly ill, just a bug. Ten minutes later her mom had gotten her a same-day appointment as a new patient with a local doctor in her college town. When she and her freshman roommate had problems, Molly's mother talked a dean into getting Molly a new housing arrangement. And when Molly called home in tears from a study abroad program to complain about a bad grade, her mom called overseas to complain directly to the professor about it. "She's a strong woman. People listen when she talks. She got me appointments with the right people," Molly said. She credited her mom's intervention for the high final grade she received. Clearly Molly had learned how effective her mother can be.

Molly's father proved equally proactive, and she was strategic about using her mom's *and* her dad's help. Her father helped prepare her for a rigorous interview for a prestigious management position. Knowing that she had to be conversant on specific financial news, he collected relevant clips daily for two weeks from the *Wall Street Journal* and sent them to her. Molly aced the interview and got the job, crediting her dad with helping prepare her. "It was a way he could contribute and feel good about it," she said.

Molly's tactic of having her dad help her in a way that would also make him feel good is something that we have heard from many students. They recognize the benefits of their parents' help, and they take advantage of that help.

Rebecca, a senior at a small liberal arts college when we first met her, had gotten plenty of help from her mother, from writing papers to tapping into her army of friends and family to help Rebecca with other class work and job opportunities. Rebecca saw nothing wrong with having mom edit her papers: "Isn't taking advantage of expertise that's available to you just *life*? In the real world it's about networking, and learning to use that."

The fact that other kids don't have the same resources as Rebecca or that so much help from mom may not be such a good idea didn't seem to bother her, at least not enough to stop asking. Besides, observed Rebecca, repeating the now-common theme, "Your parents *want* to work with you, because it's something they can help you with. It makes my mom feel good."

And Rebecca wanted to please her mom, even though their relationship has always been complicated. Her mother is reserved and Rebecca is outgoing. When she was younger Rebecca longed for the kind of mother who would hug her at the end of the school day or leave a little note in her lunch box. In college she and her mom grew very close, partly because of her newfound appreciation for her mom's networking skills and partly because being away at college lessened their once-frequent spats.

Although Rebecca's close relationship with her mother brought her a world of benefits, it also brought her a world of worry and guilt. She became dependent on her mom's inexhaustible interest in the tiniest details of her life. They talked on the cell phone and emailed each other multiple times per day. Rebecca's college friends sometimes teased her about how often she talked to her mother, and finding how much less her more independent friends talked to their moms sometimes troubled her. "Am I going to be like this with my kids? It's a good thing and a bad thing," she said, describing their close relationship. "I do wish I didn't have to think about her all the time." She describes a persistent feeling: "I didn't call her and now I feel guilty." And whenever Rebecca went home, that guilt grew— each time she felt her mom's disappointment when Rebecca visited friends rather than stay home with her.

There's always a price to pay for such intense involvement, no matter how strategically children use it or how they justify it. Molly, for example, sometimes found her mother's support smothering. Her mom was a superfan of Molly's lacrosse team. "She lives vicariously through the successes of my team and me. Sometimes her level of involvement bothers me. When someone's happiness weighs so much on you, you want to say 'Get off! I can't take the pressure!'"

Sometimes involved parents find it hard to separate themselves from their children's successes. Molly's parents assisted her every step of the way on her journey to college. They also influenced her choice of major. Describing herself as "an English major at heart," she explained wistfully that she declared a more practical major to please her parents and then chose her minor in English for herself. As Barbara's data show, this is increasingly common and not surprising in an era when college tuition has soared, but the net effect may be less ownership of the college experience by the student, less enthusiasm for learning, and less of the intellectual risk taking that promotes growth.

As parents play increasingly larger roles on campuses across America their overinvestment and its unwanted dividends are occurring more frequently. When parents hang on every grade, game, and job interview as if it were their own, and when they are able to communicate these vicarious feelings instantly via cell phone, laptop, or BlackBerry, their kids feel constantly pressured to constantly succeed. Not surprisingly some students come to resent the source of all that stress and begin to look critically at their parents and their motivations for being so involved. Students in Barbara's study expressed concern about their parents' micromanagement of their lives, about parents who wanted too much information about their academic and personal lives, and about whether parents might be too invested in their kids' successes.

Similarly, Molly worried that her mother focused too much energy on her and her siblings and not enough on herself. While she was in college her parents were contemplating a divorce, and Molly saw the link between her mother's child-centered universe and the near demise of her marriage: "Maybe she's hurt herself and us by putting so much into us. It's a double-edged sword in some ways." While Molly reaped the benefits of all her mother's efforts, she also thought it was time for her mom to get a life.

When Abby caught up with Rebecca and Molly two years later,

she found them at different ends of the spectrum, one getting closer to her mom and the other pulling away.

### Molly after College

Now in the work world, Molly is renegotiating her relationship with her mother. Her world has changed in several vital ways. She is no longer financially dependent on her parents, and her mother and father have survived their rough patch, opting to stay married. These changes have left Molly feeling less obligated to speak with her mom every day. While she certainly enjoyed talking to her mom so much in college, she always felt the tug of obligation. Now she talks less frequently with her.

Still, her parents insist that she speak to one of them at least daily. But it is usually dad whom she speaks to, and he makes the call on his drive home from work. A veteran of the corporate world, he has a new bond with his daughter, who is working for a multinational corporation. "I grew up being their friend," says Molly, and she readily shares with them personal details of her weekends that her friends won't share with their parents.

Her relationship with her mom is complex. In college Molly was ambivalent about how close she was with her mom, enjoying her unwavering support but also feeling weighed down by their intense closeness. Now that Molly no longer needs so much help and feels that her mother needs less help too, she is more distant from her mom. This can be tough on a parent who was greatly involved with her child in college and looked forward to enjoying a closer relationship after college.

### Rebecca after College

Two years later Rebecca is now working a thousand miles away from her mom in a demanding job that she loves. The difference in time zones has changed how they communicate: "When I'm finishing work, mom is going to bed. Our relationship has relied on emailing and BlackBerry messaging during the day." Calls are much harder to make, and that has been hard for Rebecca. "It's really kind of sad for me. I can't tell her when something funny happens."

Moving so far away for a job has created other changes in their relationship. "Now she sees me as more independent than I ever have been," says Rebecca. Her mother, she says, has come to respect Rebecca's passionate pursuit of her career. While some of her friends' parents may have tried to talk their kids out of taking a job so far from home, Rebecca's mom did not. "It's okay," Rebecca says. "It's not about her. It's about getting to the goal, and she respects that." Rebecca says her mother now feels less need to be so involved in ensuring her daughter's success.

Rebecca now feels less guilt about her relationship with her mom: "I think when I was in college I felt a guilt attached to talking with mom. Now it's more natural. She realizes that she needs to give me the space to come to her. Whenever I went home it was a stressor. Now I value going home so much more than ever before. When I was in college, I would go home and see my friends. My priorities have shifted and I'm more willing to spend time with mom."

According to Rebecca, she and her mom have achieved a more balanced relationship. She is aware of her mom's strengths and weaknesses: "I want to talk to her when times are good. When times are bad I need to deal with it on my own. She's not always great when times are tough." When she calls her parents now, she says, "I'm not necessarily looking for advice. I want them to relate to what I'm going through. I'm not looking for them to be like a life lesson." Her calls now have more of a give-and-take quality. "I want to know how they're doing. Have we sold the house? Who was at the party?"

If Rebecca had developed more independence in college, she and her mother might have achieved a more balanced relationship during those years. Rebecca might have been willing to spend more time with her mom, and her mom would have felt less responsible for Rebecca's success. Now the geographic distance and incompatible time zones and the barriers to communication that they pose seem to be helping Rebecca and her mom create a better relationship.

## Evolving Relationships

These close ties can be even more intense for kids of single parents, who sometimes rely on their children more than they might have if they were still married or partnered. These close relationships can create a storm of emotions for a struggling adolescent. Michael, a brilliant and sensitive student at a highly selective college, has been weathering this storm throughout his freshman and sophomore years. Tall and thin and aching with adolescent vulnerability, Michael looked like he needed mothering in the most traditional sense.

When he was in high school, according to Michael, his parents went through an awful divorce and Michael sided with his dad, cutting off all ties to his mom and eventually moving in full time with his father. For all practical purposes he now had one parent.

Michael and his father called and text-messaged each other daily. When Abby first met Michael on campus, he was just a blink away from tears. The week had been very rough; his girlfriend had just broken up with him. She was at another college, several states away, and had asked Michael to stay away. He was devastated at being unable to talk with her in person. Throughout the week his friends had rallied around him, but the greatest solace had come from his dad, who had talked at length to him every day. A decade ago processing a failing relationship with a parent was less common; it's likely that students would have talked through the breakup with friends before the weekly parent call came around. Cell phones help make this kind of conversation with parents far more common.

Michael's father traveled frequently for his job, so even when he was a high school senior Michael had spent weeks alone. Gradually their relationship evolved so that his father treated him both as a peer and a teenage son. In the summer before Michael's sophomore year, his dad had run into some money problems. He asked Michael to pitch in. Michael did so in a big way, working seventy hours a week throughout his vacation to come up with the needed cash.

Michael's dad moved back and forth, from best friend to guiding parent. "A lot of kids look at their parents as parents. Then, some look at their parents as best friends. I'm somewhere in the middle," Michael said. His dad always phoned in when he was on the road; some calls were just cheerful check-ins, but sometimes his dad was lonely and wanted to share *his* problems. Sometimes these conversations proved too draining for Michael, or they came when he was cramming for a test or hanging out with his friends. So, to avoid talking, Michael responded with a text message. Many students in our surveys reporting using text messaging in this way, keeping a connection without having to talk, giving themselves some needed space and separation.

Michael was very responsive to his father's needs and moods. Of course he loves his father and wants to help him, but self-preservation also drove him. He viewed his dad as the only adult who really knew and cared about him on a daily basis: "If you get him mad there's no one else you can go to." That reality colors their relationship. "When he asks for a favor, I try to suck it up and do it," Michael said, adding quickly that his father doesn't ask for many favors. Clearly Michael was struggling to set some boundaries. Afraid of alienating his dad and losing his support, he was also afraid to express his own needs.

Michael's dad may have been meeting his needs as much as Michael's through this contact with his son. To be fair, Michael's dad was likely worried about his divorce's impact on Michael, including his son's devastating rejection of his mom. Now Michael depended solely on his dad and so his dad may have wanted to stay in closer touch with him. Nonetheless during these transitional years to adulthood it is helpful for parents to remember to put kids' needs first and find other outlets for their own concerns. Letting them know what's going on with you is good, of course; it can help them see you as a separate individual apart from your role as a parent. But they are not yet adults, and some subjects can be inappropriate or burdensome.

## Michael's Senior Year

Two years later, when Abby visited Michael again, he told her how profoundly his relationship with his dad had changed. Throughout his sophomore year Michael and his dad had relied on each other for constant, almost instant support, even for things that weren't very important. "I expected him to always be there for me, no matter what, and that was pretty selfish of me. And he expected the same from me, no matter what was going on in my life," Michael explained. He believes that part of his dad's intense involvement in his life stemmed from his father's need to compensate for the pain caused by his divorce. For example, when Michael tried to find his own ride home for Thanksgiving among friends on campus, his father stepped in to make another arrangement. Michael found that irritating.

The summer before his junior year marked a turning point in their relationship. One morning his dad came home after a two-week business trip, exhausted after taking the red-eye. Michael, who had gotten up early to greet his dad, was tired too. Still, they sat down to talk, their shared exhaustion lowering the traditional barriers. Then Michael told his dad, "I like being there for you, when I *can* be there." His dad caught Michael's cue, and they talked honestly about the unreasonable expectations that they had both placed on their relationship. Looking back, Michael believes that the candor of their conversation allowed them both to move beyond their fears of alienating each other. While they will always be there for each other when

93

it really matters, they realize they don't need to be at each other's continual beck and call.

When Michael returned to school his father called him early in the semester, asking him what was going on, and Michael ticked off a long list of papers, tests, practices, and tournaments. "He asked me, 'What can I do?,' and I said 'Nothing.'" And that's exactly what Michael's dad did. Though they still talk regularly, they don't talk as much as they once did. As a senior, Michael is clearly much more at peace with himself. He has a new girlfriend who studied abroad with him during a junior semester. He also has begun communicating again with his mother—not a lot, but at least a little. Academically he is blooming in a very demanding major. While he describes his relationship with his dad now as a "blessing," he also recognizes its ups and downs: "There will be times when we need each other. As father and son we love each other. And as father and son, there will be times we can't stand each other and we need to do our own thing."

## The Downside of Being a Best Friend

Our interviews and studies showed that some parents think of their child as a best friend or something pretty close to it. Under this new paradigm they confide in their kids about having sex, disagreements with their spouse, intimate health issues, and finances. Not surprisingly many kids dislike this part of the arrangement.

Jessie was a junior when Abby met her. A former dancer with a passion for the arts, and a member of a popular sorority, she had lots of friends and a full social life. On the surface everything seemed to be going well for her, but in our campus interview she told a troubling story about herself and her parents.

For the past year Jessie's parents had been going through the process of divorce. Their constant calls to her had often become tirades about each other and their efforts to date other people. Jessie had a younger brother still at home, and her parents also argued about who would watch him on date nights. When Jessie went home her parents expected her to babysit. "My big problem with that is *I* was supposed to be the kid. I'm the teenager and it's my turn to live," she said.

Jessie was frustrated and angry but loved her parents deeply and expected and depended on their daily calls, even with all the tension and complaining. Her parents were nothing short of her emotional mainstays. During sophomore year, when Jessie walked in on her boyfriend and one of her friends having sex, she immediately called her parents. "To this day my mom still can't stand the guy," said Jessie, proud of her mother's support.

### Jessie after College

When Abby talked to her two years later Jessie had begun drawing some boundaries with her parents. Still in the process of getting divorced, her mother and father were at constant odds, according to Jessie. Rather than talk to each other about contentious issues (such as selling their house), they ask Jessie to act as their go-between. "It's annoying," said Jessie. "She'll say, 'Call your father and ask him this.' Now I'll say, 'You call him. I'm not your secretary.'" Through bitter experience Jessie learned that acting as their intermediary was a lose-lose situation, with each parent unleashing their anger at each other on her. Her efforts to distance herself were paying off, she said. "They don't do it as much anymore. I think they have noticed."

Jessie is still close with her parents, her dad calling several times a week and her mom every night after work, but she won't share certain things with her mom. "I've learned to not tell her about boyfriends. She's very opinionated and she might tell me something that isn't the nicest of things. I don't tell her everything and I try not to tell her about problems." Jessie also recognizes that her relationship with her mother isn't as good as it could be, at least partly tracing back to her inability to push back at her mother's upsetting calls in college. Jessie's younger brother is away at college now, and from the beginning set some boundaries with his mom. If she calls him too often he won't answer. "She knows her limits," Jessie says. "She always says, like, if she talked to him yesterday she shouldn't call for a couple of more days after that."

Now when her mom calls at an inconvenient time Jessie doesn't always answer. But her mom is persistent, and texts instead, "What's up?" While Jessie has taken tremendous steps in difficult circumstances toward adulthood, she faces a continuing battle with her mom about boundaries.

Parents can learn to read their children's cues for how much closeness they want and respond appropriately. Jessie has had to labor to draw limits that her parents could have helped create with her.

## Why Kids Can't Say No

Ironically, despite being so close, many kids can't tell their parents, at least directly, to back off. In fact only 11 percent of the students in our survey say they told their parents to stop calling so much.

Some kids are uncomfortable confronting their parents. This may come as a shock to parents who have battled teenagers on everything from curfews to picking up the wet towels left on the bathroom floor. Like us, some child experts surmise that this stems from parents assuming the role of best friend. "My gut feeling is that it's because the nature of the relationship had changed," says Suzanne Garland, a clinical psychology professor at Middlebury. "A parent is someone who is forever your parent. If you get mad and say 'Buzz off,' you know a parent will always love you. But a friend is different. There's a fear that a friendship can't sustain the kind of direct communication that a traditional parent-child relationship can."

*Drawing the Line*

Some kids do tell parents to back off, but not in so many words. Instead they set limits on when and about what they will talk to their parents. It's not just a coincidence that college students return so many of their parents' calls as they are just about to enter class or the gym. The more popular put-offs include "Sorry, I'm here, got to go now" and the familiar "Someone's on the other line. Talk to you later."

We found students using a variety of tactics to deflect parents. Some lie. Others even whisper on the phone, pretending to be in the library. Interestingly, even those students who are happy with how much they communicate with their parents admit to these deceptions, according to Barbara's research. Almost 40 percent say they are busy; 19 percent don't answer the phone. Students also find refuge from parents in technology; 14 percent resort to email, responding in their time and on their terms. Text messaging, increasingly popular, also limits the type of conversations that are possible.

Clearly the kids in this chapter love their parents and love being close to them. But there is a downside to all this intimacy, amplified by the immediacy of cell phones and computers and the yin and yang of adolescent ambivalence. Because their parents were so entwined in their lives, even at college, these kids were experiencing some disturbing feelings about themselves and their parents.

These feelings surely detracted from the students' college experience. Sarah felt dependent and less competent because she secretly relied on her dad for academic help. Having given in to her parents' constant pressure to come home from college, Shari felt resigned and regretful. Molly felt pressured by her mother's overwhelming involvement in her life. Rebecca felt guilty because even though she gladly encouraged her mother's attention, she couldn't meet her mother's need for more contact. Jessie was frustrated and angry about her new role as confidante and best friend to her divorcing parents. Michael felt stressed and anxious in part because his dad leaned on him.

When we visited them later we saw that the communication patterns established in the first years of college reverberate in the years after. On the plus side, Michael and his dad were able to build a healthier, happier relationship after realizing that they couldn't possibly be available to each other for every issue. Jessie was able to remove herself from the middle of her parents' divorce war. Rebecca too made some positive strides, thanks to her consuming passion in her work and being several time zones away from her mother. With her diagnosis of ADD, Sarah realized why she may have become so dependent on her parents and began to feel better about herself. But some of our other students were continuing to struggle in their relationships with their parents as they tried to become adults. Molly and her mother are undergoing a difficult phase, redrawing their relationship. Sarah and Rebecca are still trying to work out their identities as young adults.

## Advice for Parents

Allow your child to develop a campus life apart from you, and keep on an even keel about his or her successes and failures. Eventually children stumble when we're not there to pick them up—and they learn from it. Yet some parents seem to be trying to postpone even the first misstep as long as possible. Be cautious about expecting your child's family life to remain the priority it was in high school, which is what Shari's parents expected when they thought she would come home every weekend. Students often end up feeling guilty about this kind of burden. Going home too often also leaves less time to make new friends, an important college goal. Beware of rushing to their rescue unless it's truly necessary. Shari needed to learn on her own how to cope with the aftermath of a party; this didn't happen when her parents cleaned her room and took her home.

If you feel your child has writing difficulties, you can help by making sure he attends a college that offers support. Know the resources available, but most important, make sure your child is aware of the resources and knows how to utilize them. You can also discuss how to get other assistance and how to be assertive about seeking it; for example, some professors and teaching assistants will look over an outline or a draft of a paper during office hours. But students have to learn when and how to request this kind of assistance. A plea for help the night before a paper is due usually won't cut it, but a polite request within a reasonable time frame most likely will.

If you are a single parent make sure to find ways to meet your emotional and social needs elsewhere. Develop new friendships, join groups with common interests, and consider support groups if there is a need to discuss issues of single parenting.

If you and your child use the term "best friend" in regard to each other, as Rebecca and her mom did, consider these questions: Does my child have other best friends? Who's benefiting most from this closeness? Is it impairing her independence in any way?

Stay interested in your child's athletic and other extracurricular pursuits, of course! But learn to show your interest appropriately. Make it clear that you are attending for the pleasure of the game or the performance and that you won't go over the edge if she does a bad job on the field or onstage.

Kids who are conflicted about closeness generally have parents who have overstepped the boundaries in the relationship. This can be difficult for them to understand and even harder to change, for fear of hurting the parent. Parents need to make sure that there is closeness and warmth, but also support for growing independence.

## Chapter 6

# The Parents' Side of Being So Involved

"Being a parent is not so easy. You get messaged a lot that *you* are the single biggest risk prevention for your children in the elementary, middle, and high school years. 'Stay engaged. Stay involved. Keep the lines of communication open.' That's the message that comes from schools, churches, clinical psychologists, television shows, books, just about every quarter," says Lonnie Stonitsch, a parent in Skokie, Illinois. Happily engaged in her 9-year-old son's life, Stonitsch, 50, is also an ardent advocate for thoughtful parenting. As cochair of the Family Awareness Network of New Trier Township Schools, she organizes popular parenting talks that also speak to the parents of older kids in these college-bound communities on Chicago's affluent North Shore.

"Parents think part of the magic bullet is to stay engaged," she says, barely taking a breath before continuing. "There's disapproval of the parent who isn't involved." The pressure to protect their kids, help them achieve academic success, and win their peers' approval has encouraged parents to become deeply involved in their children's daily lives, and this pattern reverberates into the college years and beyond.

Even though her son is young, Stonitsch is looking toward his future. Through her work promoting more mindful and less stressful parenting, she has gotten to know parents with kids in or en route to college, and she feels their pain and is anticipating a bit of her own. "So when you get accepted at college, you turn off all those things? It's a big switch to turn off. Now you expect me to send them to school and never talk to them?"

In just a few passionate paragraphs Stonitsch captures some of the most important feelings and forces that drive iConnected parents' behavior and relationships with their kids. The feelings that characterize these parents don't suddenly develop when kids head off to college. These beliefs take root much earlier.

"Good" parents believe that they must always be involved in their children's lives and available to them. If they aren't, they fear that their kids won't do as well in school and that they'll be more vulnerable to any number of perils. As a result many parents often feel anxious. Adding to their anxiety is pressure from their peers: "good" parents are accepted by their peers, while those who fail to fit that definition usually aren't. On the brighter side, many parents feel much closer to their kids than their parents were to them, which is a source of joy to them. Not surprisingly, they take satisfaction in their parenting.

In this chapter we trace how these feelings emerge and the cultural forces that contribute to them, as we hear from parents and educators of younger students, as well as college parents from Abby's interviews and Barbara's survey of Middlebury moms and dads. Understanding the psychology behind iConnecting behavior can help parents understand why they act the way they do and how to be more effective parents before, during, and after the college years.

## Cultural Forces

*Postponing Parenthood, Fewer Kids, Passionate Parenting*
The forces that helped create iConnected parenting have been building for years. Over the past several decades people have been choosing to have fewer children and are having them at a later stage in life. With fewer children, parents are able to focus more intently on them. After waiting so long to have kids, many parents approach their roles with the pleasure and purpose of Ms. Stonitsch.

Even though parents tend to be older when they have their kids, many are also healthier and more committed to fitness at midlife than were the generations before them. Today moms and dads often join kids in their pursuits, coaching the soccer or baseball team, going on bike rides, hikes, and camping trips. Abby's husband J.D. learned to ski in his late 40s, and Abby herself returned to the slopes a few years earlier to keep up with their snowboarding son Jack and his equally fearless younger brother, Carlos. Many parents have a sense that they are just not as old as those who were in the same station of life generations ago. Fifty is now the new 40, 60 the new 50, and with exercise and a healthful diet these older moms and dads are waging a vigorous campaign against time.

Parents want their children to succeed, and though their definitions of success may vary, they are devoted to their overall goal. Their dedication translates into parental involvement. Indeed in Barbara's survey of Middlebury parents, two-thirds reported being more involved in their kids' lives than their parents were with them. The scale of parents' engagement differs and depends on a variety of factors. Overall the message for parents to stay engaged is heard now in nearly every community, including those for whom college is a hope, not a given.

This generation of parents is also far more likely to have gone to college than their own parents, and is comfortable seeking advice from diverse sources. Besides Dr. Spock's *Baby and Child Care*, there were far fewer parenting resources available for parents of Baby Boomers. Today, Amazon.com lists more than twelve thousand books in its parenting category. In addition, parenting videos, magazines, articles, and television shows such as *Nanny 911* and *Supernanny* give even more advice. Parenting experts are regulars on the television morning talk-show circuit; lectures such as Stonitsch's are a huge draw. A talk by Harvard professor Howard Gardner, author of several books on "multiple intelligences," drew an audience of nine hundred on a Thursday night, testament to parents' deep desire to hone their child-raising skills.

The thirst for knowledge about good parenting doesn't end when kids step on campus. Barbara's workshop for first-year parents at Middlebury, "Remaining Connected While Fostering Autonomy: The Challenges of Parenting During the College Years," draws a crowd. Parents want to learn how much to be involved in the day-to-day lives of their newly enrolled kids. Many have been heavily engaged for so long that scaling down their habit of involvement is intimidating.

*Carpools, Hockey Moms, and More Chances to Bond*
With fewer kids than earlier generations, parents are also working more, with many moms returning to work within a few years after the birth of their children. One way for parents to stay involved in their kids' lives is through their scheduled activities (hence the "soccer mom"). Carting children to sports practices and dance and music lessons and attending their performances and games help parents bond more tightly with their kids. Bumper stickers and decals of miniature lacrosse, hockey, and basketball players announce their dedication. Many parents find genuine joy in watching their kids play and perform. In some cases, though, these activities can take over a family life, especially when parents begin to live vicariously through their kids.

Recently this intense kind of involvement and the hectic schedules that are its hallmark have begun to be widely criticized. "The Growing Backlash against Overparenting" was a 2009 *Time* magazine cover story, quickly picked up by other news outlets. Like this one mom Abby interviewed, some parents are hearing the call: "You try to get a play date with someone—and don't even get me started on travel sports—they have travel hockey, piano lessons, and when the hell do they eat dinner? 'If they were sitting home, they would be bored,' the mom says. Who is making all these plans? For a seven-year-old they are driving to Wisconsin for a hockey game. *Travel hockey* for these people—that's a death sentence. Travel hockey lasts nine months!"

This is a very different viewpoint from that of a college student's mom, who saw hockey as a way to bond with her daughter and make some new friends along the way. Leslie's daughter, Katie, began hockey lessons at age 5 (along with karate and art courses) and fell in love with the sport. In the early years Leslie logged countless hours with Katie, traveling to practices, games, and tournaments. In high school, as Katie chased her dream to play for a prestigious Division III college, she made scores of overnight road trips to weekend hockey games and competitions, accompanied by her mom. Even though Leslie views herself as a traditional authority-figure mother (one who chose to stay home with her kids) she compares her relationship to Katie as that of a best friend.

Over the years Leslie found a lot of support among her peers for her involved style of parenting. Becoming involved in their kids' activities creates new friendships and other social networks, which in turn help sustain their involvement. Going on the road with Katie was fun, Leslie said, partly because of the other hockey parents. "When you go away for a weekend, there's dinner and drinks in the hotel at night. It's a social outlet for the adults." Katie's departure for college was rough for Leslie. "It's kind of the same thing as when your best friend moves away to a new and more exciting life and you're left there holding the bag," she says.

But the patterns established in high school often extend into college. Leslie became a college hockey parent, attending games and tournaments, even overseas. And this helped ease the loss she felt.

Some parents with resources travel considerable distances to play the superfan role for the college students in their lives, which seems to happen everywhere that there are parents with enough money and interest to follow their children's athletic and artistic pursuits. At Davidson College in North Carolina a school official says affluent parents often buy condos on a nearby lake so they can regularly attend their students' games or performances.

Lacrosse, soccer, music, theater, dance, Scouts—all these activities and more are supported by a community of parents who encourage each other's continued participation, from preschool through college. Some families engage in these activities to enhance their child's chances for admission to college, which can help, but not as much as some parents think.

## The Long Road to College Admissions

Parents' efforts to improve their child's chances for college admission have increased dramatically over the past fifteen years because there were more applicants than ever. This has been most visible in families whose kids are striving for admission to the most competitive schools, or whose parents are doing the actual striving for these admissions and all they represent. "The ultimate suburban legend is that where you go to college determines your success," said James W. Jump, president of the National Association for College Admission Counseling. "There are parents who are more focused on the name on the sticker on the back of the SUV than the quality of the educational experience." Sometimes this produces an unhappy result. "The sad situation is when the prestige of the institution overrides the fit of another institution," said Katy Murphy, director of college counseling at Bellarmine College Preparatory School in San Jose, California.

"Some kids will go to college and endure it. But I want them to love it. Sometimes they endure it for a year and sacrifice themselves in terms of flunking out or transferring, and sometimes they graduate."

But families applying to middle of the road and much less selective schools also feel some heat. "Most stories in the media focus on top schools and how competitive they are," Jump said. "That attention has had a trickle-down effect. The subtle message that gets out is college is difficult to get into and that ratchets up the pressure on every student regardless of the school that they are trying to get into. It makes parents anxious and then students anxious too."

This push to get into college begins well before high school, turning up the temperature on kids' performances in school and in the community. In well-to-do towns an ambitious minority of parents postpone sending their capable kids to kindergarten in order to give them an edge—for college. As she reported in a story for the *New York Times*, Abby explored this practice in Connecticut's most prosperous towns. Parents' dedication to their kids' education is not a regional phenomenon, however. Throughout the country well-intentioned moms and dads dive into their kids' schoolwork as if it were their own. And they jockey for the volunteer slots in classrooms and on field trips in order to stay close to their kids as well as to form useful relationships with teachers. At many elementary schools parents lobby behind the scenes to have their child placed with a popular teacher or to make sure he is in a class with friends and students who won't disrupt his learning.

Some schools are actively resisting this surge of parental involvement. In an affluent neighborhood of Portland, Oregon, Llewellyn Elementary School's principal, Steve Powell, has clearly defined what's appropriate at Llewellyn: "We discourage parents from micromanaging." While Powell appreciates the contribution of parent volunteers in the classroom, his school limits it. "We're instructing children. We're not going to manage parents," he said in a phone interview.

And homework? "Homework is for the child, not for the parent," said Powell, who has been educating kids for more than thirty years.

Later, in an email, Powell explained his stance: "My job is to teach children to become autonomous learners. By autonomous learner I mean that they need to be able to think for themselves." He and many other educators and child experts believe children learn best by making a mistake and reflecting on that mistake with adult guidance and in a nurturing, caring environment.

"I don't want to give the impression that we delight in having children fail," Powell wrote. "We want students to experience more success than failure. But I believe that we now live in a society that never wants children to suffer, experience pain, or fail at anything. That is not going to bode well for them in the future. Children need to learn all of life's lessons at the appropriate age to develop into strong, caring, and autonomous adults. We coddle children way too much. Children need to be let loose (again at the appropriate age and with adults monitoring) to make their own mistakes and learn from them. We should not abandon them but we need to let them go so they can experience life. Children will never become competent adults if we constantly monitor their every move and clean up their mistakes."

Despite the efforts of educators like Steve Powell, parents continue to intervene at school to help improve their children's chances for the far-off goal of college.

Years ago parental involvement cooled off in high school. Now it heats up in high schools full of college hopefuls. Parents with money hire tutors for every conceivable subject, press colleagues for internships for their kids, and find summer programs to boost credentials, in a marathon effort to produce desirable transcripts for their children. This often culminates in parents crossing the line in their assistance with the college application process. High school guidance counselors report that parents often use online portals that are meant for students and college admissions staff. For example, parents at

Mount St. Mary Academy in Little Rock, Arkansas, sometimes call Tricia Davis, the school's counselor, to report that a college hasn't received their child's high school transcript, information gleaned online using their child's password. "A lot of kids' parents contact us, although not as much as when I was in Florida and Nashville," she said, referring to her previous positions in other schools. In Connecticut, Sheila Nussbaum, a counselor at Hall High School, said, "I'm amazed at how much parents are doing. They'll call and say, 'I'm filling out an application for GW [George Washington University] and I have a question.'" When Nussbaum asks why the student isn't filling out the application, they'll say "He's too busy." This response dismays many counselors, partly because the kid isn't taking ownership of the college application, and partly for what it portends for the student's future. "If they can't fill out their application, how are they going to fill out their tax form or apply for a mortgage?" asks Katy Murphy at Bellarmine College Preparatory School. "It's a life skill," she said.

In response college admissions officers continue to seek ways to make sure applicants' work is their own. The new writing portion of the SAT, for example, is a better window on a student's writing skills than the admissions essay that can be edited by parents or paid advisors. Some families might rethink the college application process, especially those who say "we" are applying to college, a telltale sign of overinvolved parenting. Kids need to be responsible for the process, own their choices, and do the work. Parents can be wonderful sounding boards, sources of advice, and companions on college tours, but they are not the ones to complete the forms, arrange for references, or write the essay. Autonomy builds more engagement by the student in the long run and is important in the college application process.

However, parental guidance is important in explaining the family's financial picture and how it influences a student's choice of colleges. Having that conversation early on can be beneficial and can help the student take a step toward adulthood. Most college students graduate with loans, yet some with whom we've talked are unaware of the implications, or the amounts. They can be brought into this discussion much earlier. Financially, parents at this point may look forward to paying off college tuition and focusing on building retirement funds. Although many kids are working during college and taking on their own loans, some parents may spare them from any burdens at all, even jeopardizing their own future. Our research shows that the more financially dependent students are on their parents, the less close they think they are to adulthood.

## The Rising Price of College

One of the most powerful elements driving parental involvement is the cost of college education. From 1982–2007 the price of college increased 439 percent, according to *Measuring Up 2008*, a report by the National Center for Public Policy and Higher Education; in contrast, over the same span, median family income rose 147 percent. For many families, the price of a college education is growing out of reach. The report showed the net cost (tuition, room and board, minus financial aid) for a public, four-year university equal to about 28 percent of the average family income; for its private counterpart, 76 percent of average family income. Hardest hit have been low- and middle-income families. The poorest families handed over 55 percent of their income for public colleges and universities (after accounting for all student financial aid)— a rise from 39 percent in 2000. Families squarely in the middle income range shelled out 25 percent of their income (up from 18 percent in 2000), and those with the highest income (top 20 percent of the population) paid 9 percent of their income (up from 7 percent in 2000).

Even those who can afford such prices are exasperated. One popular joke compares the price of a private college education to driving a brand-new luxury car off a cliff, four years in a row.

When parents call Jane Martindell, dean for academic advising at Kenyon College in Ohio, about a problem their child is having, their opening salvo, regardless of the problem, frequently includes a reference to their financial outlay. "I'm not paying forty thousand dollars a year to see blah, blah happen," repeats Martindell, who is alternately wearied by the constant plaint and sympathetic about the situation.

The knowledge of how much their parents are paying for college can push students to care more about grades than learning and to please their parents more than themselves. This is neither a healthy path to adulthood nor a good return on a sizable investment. Some parents expect their children to contribute a portion of their tuition, even in cases where it is not essential financially, in order to increase the kids' commitment and investment.

At some point it is important to recognize that your children need a life that is personally fulfilling and to trust their instincts to find it. Barbara's son enjoys teasing her about her own worries when he expressed interest in abandoning computer science for psychology. She remembers how secure computer science had seemed as a career. But he wasn't enjoying it at all and was far more interested in the people part of computing than the hardware or software side. Just a few years out of college her son is an analyst who studies social media and consumer intelligence and advises companies how to use the results. This is certainly not work either of them could have foreseen, but his social science research skills and love of technology blended into an ideal job, and both of them know that he would have been pretty miserable as a computer engineer. Similarly she was wistful when her math whiz daughter abandoned the field for political science and a business minor, but marvels now at how she employs those math skills as a campaign finance guru, with four successful congressional campaigns behind her and considerable consulting experience.

### The Fuel of Anxiety

Many parents feel compelled to monitor their kids because they see the world as a more dangerous place for children than when they were kids themselves. In the past twenty years there has been increased coverage of child tragedies: abductions, sexual abuse, and murders. Many parents are afraid to allow their children to walk unescorted, even very short distances to school or team practices. Parents use an array of technologies to protect and connect with their kids. "Nanny-cams" secretly tape babysitters; as children venture out into the world, nervous parents outfit them with global positioning bracelets and locator devices in case they go missing; some parents buy their kids cell phones equipped with GPS chips. Some summer camps now provide daily email updates and webcams of campers for anxious parents, while others struggle to ban cell phones and email, hoping to create the sense of independence that camps have traditionally provided. Many parents use their cell phones to keep tabs on their kids. From conversations in the grocery store to websites on the Internet, parents hear constantly about reasons for concern. Substance abuse, suicide, eating disorders, bullying, cyberstalking, teen pregnancy, and sexually transmitted diseases are now a part of the national conversation. The terrorist attacks of September 11 have also taken their toll on parents' psyches. Middle schools, high schools, and colleges are no longer considered safe after the massacres at Columbine, Virginia Tech, McGill, and Northern Illinois University instilled worry and fear, in spite of the fact that kids are more likely to be hit by lightning than a bullet from a crazed classmate. On Abby's recent tours of colleges with her son Jack, tour guides made a point of showing the emergency call boxes across the campus landscape; displaying blue lights, the call boxes link to campus security.

### The Push to Be Happy Creates More Involvement and Less Resilience

Some parents are so anxious about their kids' well-being and so wrapped up in their lives that they can't bear to see them unhappy, even for a moment. Again and again in our personal and professional lives we have had parents tell us they just want their kids to be happy. In American culture happiness is a common theme. Books, magazine articles, news stories, and seminars on how to get and stay happy are nearly everywhere.

Some experts say there's a danger in such a focus on happiness. Author and psychologist Aaron Cooper warns about the perils of this trend. Parents simply can't keep their kids perpetually happy; it's impossible. Parents who want only the best for their kids need to realize that kids need to achieve happiness on their own. Just as important, kids need to learn to roll with life's ups and downs. They can't do that if parents always rush in to soothe the slightest discomfort. They also can't learn how to solve their own problems if mom and dad always do it for them; ironically this actually robs them of the happiness that comes from fixing one's own problems. It can also lead to learned helplessness if they think they don't have the power to address these issues themselves.

## Parenting in the College Years

### Peer Pressure Parent-Style

The peer pressure to be involved that parents experienced in their child's earlier years is still present in the college years. When one of Abby's friends dropped her son off for his first year at college she intended to stay only one day. But she changed her mind when she learned that other parents were staying longer, some to make sure their kids got into the right courses. If she left, Patty thought, she might put her son, her first child to go to college, at a disadvantage relative to other students.

Sometimes the pressure surfaces indirectly, through the child. One professor at a New England liberal arts college had raised her children to be independent. When her first child went off to college, the mom deliberately let her set the pace on when and how to communicate. She did the same when another child left for college, but when she came home for Christmas she moped around the house, the mom said. Finally the daughter told her mom what was bothering her: "All my friends' moms call them every day." The mom was shocked. "I didn't know that you wanted me bugging you," the mom said. When her daughter returned to school the mom did what her daughter asked, although they actually ended up speaking every other day. "Now she calls me 'mommy.' It's sort of a joke, especially if she's in front of her friends, showing off that she has a close relationship with her mother," the mom said.

Parents may want to band together to convey to their kids that there are many ways of showing their caring and that they don't have to talk every day for this to be evident or make a lengthy extended stay out of a brief orientation session. The social norming that takes place among kids can also affect parents, who get caught up in the instant accessibility and constant involvement shown by their friends and peers.

### Closer and More Satisfying Relationships

Kids and their parents today are closer in many ways than in past generations, and this easier intimacy continues into the college years and beyond, sustained by texts, calls, emails, and Facebook. Now students are more likely to invite their parents into their daily lives. Marilyn works at a large Midwestern university, where her two older children have gone to school. As a single parent she is also very close to her kids, although definitely not their best friend. "There's one thing I think that is cool: they allow me to be part of their friends' lives," she said, describing their relationship. For example, she said, "All of my son's friends seem to think that I am their stepmother." When her son was inducted into a fraternity on campus he asked his mom to come

113

to the formal ceremony, an unusual invitation for a parent, according to Marilyn. Parents like Marilyn embrace these close relationships. In fact when she is sometimes incredulous about how her children let her into their lives, her friends say, "Don't look a gift horse in the mouth!"

Parents in Barbara's Middlebury survey and in Abby's reporting said their kids welcomed this closeness. One dad of a sophomore noted, "I don't feel my daughter has the need to distance herself from me that I felt toward my parents."

Overall, parents have told us, and we have found in our own lives, how much more reciprocal parents' relationships are with their kids today, and how this affectionate give-and-take has drawn everyone closer. Observed one Middlebury parent, "We are closer because I think I am more accepting and less judgmental of her actions and choices and perhaps because I share more of my life."

A new candor on both sides also characterizes these relationships. One parent in Barbara's survey wrote, "[My daughter] and many of her friends feel free to confide in me and my friends about everything, including their sex lives. It's a totally new day." Students whom Abby interviewed also said they confided in their parents even about sex. "I tell my mom stuff. I went out with a guy and he told me 'Mr. Pokey' wants to come out and play. My friends were like, 'How could you tell your mom that?'" said one young college student, who still laughed at her date's clumsy pass. Her friends' reactions show, as does our reporting and research, that not all students are so frank with their parents. Parents too may get carried away with the new candor. As we learned in chapter 4, sometimes parents share too much information about their personal lives for their kids' comfort level, and parents need to be aware of this.

How parents respond when their kids begin to share more is critical to the health of the relationship and how well these late adolescents navigate the transition to adulthood. Giving them enough space, helping them create boundaries, and respecting their privacy will help build a healthy relationship.

### Parents Are More Empathetic

Perhaps because parents have been so involved from the earliest years in their children's lives they tend to feel more empathy for their children's stresses. Just listen to parents talk about the competition of college admissions. A common refrain heard among parents who are college graduates is "Today I could never get into the college that I attended." They worry about how stressful it must be if their child is applying somewhere equally competitive. The rising cost of college also concerns most parents, who worry about burdening their kids with years of college loans in our dramatically altered economy.

The financial pressure and intense competition to achieve in college resonated with the Middlebury parents, who compared it to their own college experience. "College was cheaper. There was less pressure to achieve great things. Now I know how much competition this generation faces," wrote one parent. Parents might try expressing their empathy so that their children feel less pressure, saying something like "I know it is hard to get a summer job in the current economy and I appreciate all you are doing to find one."

### Happiness and Sadness

Most parents experience mixed emotions when their children leave home for college. They are sad to see their kids go, but they are happy to see them reach the college mecca. Parents have spent years preparing their kids for this great moment, but in some cases they haven't prepared themselves for how they will manage it.

Kirk Manning is vice president of student life and dean for student development at St. Thomas Aquinas College and previously was associate provost and dean of students at Widener University. He is well acquainted with this scenario: "I think that some parents are really ready for students to go off to college and have developed some kind of plan, and I have parents who haven't." At Widener Manning gave this typical talk to parents during first-year orientation: "There's still time for you to pursue your dreams, not just an extension of your son's or daughter's but your own dreams." Typically parents' reactions were mixed. "It's great to read the faces," he said. "Some are nodding happily and others are starting to well up with tears. Some are really looking forward to it and some are just devastated. Their whole identity is tied up in their kids."

When a child leaves for college it is a huge change for the whole family—the child, siblings, parents, even grandparents. For parents who are living through their kids or are used to managing their every move, this may be an even tougher transition. Even though they may cling to their kids electronically, they will no longer see their kids on a daily basis. Some parents find it hard to let their kids separate from them and begin making their own decisions.

On the other hand, parents who have been planning for this change may be able to experience more joy for their kids and themselves. Of course they will miss their kids and feel a loss as they set one less place at the dinner table, but they will not be consumed by it. With a little more space to explore their interests some parents enjoy this new freedom. Knowing this is such a significant adjustment for the family, parents may want to plan ahead and prepare themselves for when their child leaves for college. Building new interests, expanding social contacts, volunteering in your community, mentoring young people in local schools or in your job, or taking on a new project at work can all fill what might seem like a large void.

### Optimism and Ambivalence

Midlife is often when careers peak and people look forward to investing more in their professional and personal lives. Today, with new attitudes towards aging, some parents see a vibrant future. Just listen to the 53-year-old parents of a Clark University student: "Physically we're not that much younger than our parents were at this stage. But in terms of our view of the world and what the future will bring, we have more of a sense of possibility. We don't have this view of the future that you just settle into it and decrepitude. It's the sense that we are still growing. There's travel and education."

With the kids finally safely away at college, parents think they will have a chance to reconnect with each other. Or not. A popular commercial for an erectile dysfunction drug shows a middle-aged couple about to have some fun of their own when their daughter arrives home unexpectedly from college for the weekend. The parents' faces show a mixture of surprise, disappointment, and pleasure at seeing their laundry-toting daughter. (Thank goodness the pill is the long-acting type.)

The image of the couple with their little pill is now rivaling that of the weepy mom with the empty nest. Researchers who study midlife have found this to be one of the more satisfying times of life, in part because some of the burdens of parenting have lifted and the period of parenting adolescents, typically the most stressful, has now passed.

In many cases parents of college students today lack some of the freedoms that this stage of life once offered, as the electronic tether works both ways. Although parents may get a kick out of hearing from their kids about some fleeting excitement, they may also be irritated at being expected to be available around the clock. The constant contact also sustains a sense that parenting is still a daily responsibility, which was not how parents likely felt when their kids left home in the era of the weekly phone call.

Some critics have dubbed this phenomenon of parenting post-adolescent children "permaparenting." In a downward economic climate, with more kids boomeranging back home to live, it seems to be a growing trend that can extend well into the early adult years. This is occurring in other countries as well, as Barbara learned when

117

she was interviewed by a reporter from *Veja*, the Brazilian equivalent of *Newsweek*, for their story on "kangaroo kids," those who are back in the parental pocket in their 20s and 30s. While on sabbatical in Japan she also observed firsthand the "parasite single" problem, in which some young adults live at home well into their 30s, a problem that is also prominent in Italy and the United Kingdom. The trick for parents seems to be to learn how to manage the level of involvement in a way that neither infantilizes the young adult nor strips the parent of newfound freedoms.

Parents who are still deeply involved with their kids during college may want to figure out how to reconcile this time commitment with what their expectations are for their own lives at this point. While it is a pleasure to spend time with growing adult children you see less often, that is quite different from still being the one on call to fill and mail prescriptions or edit the paper that's due tomorrow morning. Parents need a life too, and it's reasonable to figure out how to put boundaries in place that acknowledge this. It's healthy for your child to know more about your other roles and their value and importance and about how to take over these tasks for himself. ("No, I can't fill and mail that prescription for you, but you can call the pharmacy and have it transferred to one near you. I'm at work and can't get to the pharmacy and post office.")

## Technology

All of these forces—demographics, the desire for children' success and perpetual happiness, and peer pressure—have created a culture of involved parents. And the ubiquity of cell phones and computers encourages and enables moms and dads to parent with even greater intensity, whether their children sleep in the crib or in a dorm room hundreds of miles from home.

Over the past decade cell phone ownership has grown explosively among young and adult callers. The unlimited calling and family plans, introduced just a few years back, have helped accelerate that growth. In 2000 only 33 percent of college students had cell phones, according to the research organization Student Monitor. Mostly, the phones were probably purchased by parents for use while students were traveling to and from school or in emergencies. By 2004, 90 percent of students had cell phones, Student Monitor reported. Students were using them every day in decidedly nonemergency situations. ("Hey, what's up? Where we gonna meet for lunch?") In a move meant to save money and acknowledge students' preference for cell phones, colleges have also been pulling out landlines.

Students who arrive on campus today have lived in a cell phone universe, some getting their own phones in middle or elementary school. A 2010 report from the Pew Internet & American Life Project shows a sharp rise in preteen and adolescent ownership. Eighteen percent of 12-year-olds owned cell phones in 2004. By 2009, 58 percent of 12-year-olds had their own phones.

The survey also showed an increase in ownership by age; for example, 64 percent of 17-year-olds owned a cell phone in 2004, compared to 83 percent in 2009. There were differences in ownership according to socioeconomic status, with affluent teens more likely to own a phone than those from families less well-off. Kids in elementary schools also are part of the trend, and peer pressure plays a big role. Recently several students in Abby's son Carlos's fifth-grade class got their own cell phones, and now Carlos has begun a relentless campaign to get one too, writing and tirelessly singing new lyrics to the classic "Frère Jacques": 'I want a cell phone, I want a cell phone. Yes, I do. Yes I do.'" The trend reaches young students in economically disadvantaged areas. Dr. Renee Hobbs, a professor at Temple University and expert in media literacy education, has researched how students from kindergarten through eighth grade in poor, urban communities use media and technology and how it affects their literacy and academic development. At the Russell Byers Charter School in Philadelphia, where more than 70 percent of students qualify for free or reduced lunches, nearly 80 percent of the students had their own cell phones by the third grade, she said.

Parents were somewhat slower to use cell phones than their kids, and more tentative with the technology, especially text-messaging. As of 2009 the Pew study showed that 83 percent of American adults have some form of cell phone, up from 65 percent in 2004. This number is expected to continue growing, while landline use continues to plummet.

The swift flow of information between parents and kids creates more opportunities for parents to intervene on their children's behalf, from middle school through graduate school, and not always in a positive way.

Even though a good number of schools ban cell phones during the class day, kids still use them. Again and again Abby heard the same scenario from high school administrators: upset over a bad grade or some other issue, a student sneaks into a bathroom with a cell, contacts his parents, who then immediately calls the teacher, department chair, or even the school principal before the end of class. (In some schools, such as New Trier High School on Chicago's North Shore, students are now allowed to text in the halls and make calls in the vestibules.) Dr. Don Slater, a principal at Hall High School in West Hartford, Connecticut, was on the receiving end of one of those calls when he called a student to his office for allegedly using profanity during a school soccer game. Before he could talk to the student the father was already on Dr. Slater's line asking, "Why is my son being called to your office?" At Mount St. Mary Academy, an all-girls Catholic high school in Little Rock, students caught with cell phones are fined $25 the first time. "The second time they are completely confiscated," Davis said. The academy has an economically diverse enrollment, and one would think the fine might stop all the texting. But that hasn't happened, according to Davis. "We frequently have situations in which a parent will call and say, 'My kid made an "F" on a test.' And we say, 'How do you know that?' And they say, 'My kid just texted me from class.' Or the kid gets in trouble and mom will call me to rescue the child from discipline office." How did the mom know? Her child texted her.

During the same period social networking bloomed, even though there was a lag between kids' and parents' usage, just as there was initially with cell phone adoption. Facebook, launched in 2004 (from a Harvard dorm room), was available only to people with college and university email addresses until 2006. At that time there were 12 million users; the number had grown to 400 million by 2010, with more than 50 percent of U.S. members being age 35 or older. Twitter, the social networking tool that permits short updates (140 characters maximum), made its debut only in 2006, and by 2009 was the third most popular social networking site, although its use was less common among students. Today cell phones, laptops, email, texting, smartphones, Twitter, Facebook, and blogs are a part of life, but this has happened so rapidly and continues to evolve so fast that some parents haven't caught up psychologically.

This frequent contact between parent and child has created and amplified powerful feelings among parents. Many parents are anxious because they feel compelled to be involved and perpetually available for their kids via cell phone or computer and feel guilty if they are not. A good number also feel an overwhelming sense of personal investment in their kids, fed by this virtual connection.

Of course, in the past, parents did worry about their kids, but they weren't receiving texts at work from their kids, upset about a grade in middle school math or a run-in with a high school coach. When their kids went off to college, parents might have felt the usual concerns. Would their kid make friends, manage tough classes, or ever change their sheets? But without a daily commentary about selfish roommates, difficult courses, and unfair coaches, parents then were able to keep their involvement and anxiety at tolerable levels. Today that's much harder to do. It's an insidious cycle: heightened anxiety, coupled with the expectation of getting a prompt response to calls, texts, and emails, breeds impatience, which in turn feeds anxiety.

In the past parents experienced a feeling of relief that once kids were safely away at college a significant part of their parenting had been successfully completed. Without a virtual connection, it was easier to feel this way. Parents couldn't supervise their kids' study schedule during exam week or make sure they weren't overdoing it at a keg party. They could, though, reignite their marriage and reinvent their careers. And as for their kids, parents could enjoy a deeper relationship with them as they treated them more as adults and less as children in need of constant oversight. Today this sense of relief and satisfaction in a task well done are harder to come by as parents try to keep managing their kids' lives via cell phone and computer. It's also more difficult to achieve when parents derive so much satisfaction and identity as a "good parent" who constantly fixes their kids' problems and is revered by other parents for doing so.

Part of this need to fix stems from years of habit and often kids' expectations of their parents' involvement even in the college years and beyond. Part of it also comes from the potent influence of other involved parents. Our ever-present cell phones have helped sustain it.

*Always Involved, Always Available, Thanks to Technology*
Wireless technology enables parents to stay closely connected to their kids and feeds parents' desire for deeper involvement in their children's lives. With cell phones, this involvement can lead to a feeling that parents must be available every second of the day to take their child's text or call, no matter what their child's age. Naturally, because they are engaged and loving parents, they may try to fix whatever problem

surfaces in the call or text. In the child's early years the problem may be as simple as "Mom, I forgot my math homework. Can you bring it to school?" The parent knows that if she doesn't drop off his homework, he may get docked a grade. Because she wants him to do well at school, she interrupts her day (if she can) and brings it. Of course this doesn't help the child in the long run to remember to pack his homework in his backpack the night before school. For many parents this cycle of involvement, accessibility, and rescuing continues well into college and beyond, and educators and even employers are well versed in it. Now schools and companies are struggling with how to address it.

DOONESBURY ©2006 G. B. Trudeau. Reprinted with permission of UNIVERSAL UCLICK. All rights reserved.

Sometimes these texts and calls are almost automatic. "A lot of these kids don't even realize they are flipping open the phone and calling mom. It's like breathing," said Dr. Timothy Dohrer, principal of the Winnetka campus of New Trier High School, a highly ranked school. Dohrer is developing programs that teach kids to be more aware of their behavior and to learn how to calm themselves instead of speed-dialing mom or dad. He also encourages parents to resist rushing in to solve their child's momentary crisis. "Communication between parents and kids would be okay, if parents wouldn't take it to the next level, if parents would just let it go. You don't have to fix it. That's what sets up this negative situation." Instead Dohrer encourages parents to be less reactive when their children call with problems that they can solve themselves. "Parents need to step back and say 'I'm going to listen and support and allow my child to make the decision here.'"

Some parents do break the cycle. One suburban mom had her "Aha" moment when her high school daughter called because she had forgotten to bring her team uniform shirt to school for a game that day. "She wanted to know 'What should I do?' I said, 'What do you mean what should you do? Think about what you should do. Should you ask a friend to borrow one? Should you talk to the coach? Figure it out.' She was annoyed that I was so quick to dismiss her question." But before the shirt incident the mom had seen a pattern forming that she didn't like. "This phone was part mommy-by-extension, that I was available twenty-four hours a day no matter what. When she would call for a ride, she would then call back again a few minutes later when I was trying to leave the house and put the dog inside. I would say, 'I'm going to be there. What are you calling for?'"

The likely answer is that the daughter wanted her mom to be constantly available to solve her problems and ease her moments of anxiety and boredom. The mom, though, thought that was unhealthy. "It was at a stage where, if I had let it go on. . . . I hear of stories of daughters calling mom on the way to class in college. I don't think they should talk twelve times per day to mom when they are twenty. A healthy separation is a really important thing."

Even parents who seem to have healthy relationships with their independent kids are not immune to this sense of obligation to make themselves available on their cell phone around the clock. "I would be lying if I didn't say I have made my husband go back inside the house to get my cell phone," said the mom, who has one kid at the University of Minnesota, one kid in high school, and two more out of college and on their own. Her vigilance stems from a concern that she be available for them when something goes wrong, but it also comes from a positive place. She loves her kids and wants to share in their good news too.

Parents might feel a lot less anxious if they allowed themselves to be a little less available and gradually shifted more of the responsibility for their children's daily lives to their children, in age-appropriate stages. Teaching children to be responsible not only for doing their homework but for putting it in their backpack immediately afterward is a good step toward building self-reliance. Having kids plan ahead for game days by knowing their schedules and making sure uniforms are clean and in the right place is another step that can begin, even in the early school years. These small efforts and others like it can create positive behaviors that carry over into college and the workforce.

## Impatience: Parents Too Want Instant Gratification

Our wireless world creates an expectation in all generations of instant contact, anywhere, anytime, anyplace. Stepping back and waiting patiently is often a hard thing for parents to do when they can have instant entrée through technology to educators and, in the years before college, to their kids' grades. Our culture's emphasis on achieving high grades at every age makes it even harder.

Today a growing number of middle and high schools employ online programs that allow access via a password to a student's latest homework, quiz, and test scores. Some schools provide the password only to students; others give it to parents too. Lisa Goodwin taught middle school students in Willington, Connecticut: "Parents would call me as soon as I would post a grade. My response was 'I just posted the grade. Your child hasn't received the paper back and I will be discussing it with your daughter or son.'" She urged parents to talk about the assignment first with their kids. "It was like they cut the kid completely out of the conversation, even though it was the kid's grade." Eventually the school adjusted the program so that students could see their grades before their parents did. Parents' heavy focus on grades also affected the students. "I would see a lot of anxiety with kids over grades. They would say, 'I don't think B- is a good grade,'

Mrs. Goodwin said." Meanwhile, parents were missing opportunities to teach their kids that it was unrealistic to expect an A in every subject or that students need to plan ahead and develop study skills."

The increase in parents' calls and emails and their expectation of a speedy response has accelerated the tempo of school life. If parents can't reach a counselor, teacher, or principal directly, they often leave a message, noting their cell phone number. With cell phones in their pocket or pocketbook, parents are *always* available for teachers' calls. As a result many educators in elementary, middle, and high school are struggling to answer a steadily growing queue of parent emails about grades and other concerns, in addition to preparing lesson plans, teaching, grading tests and papers, correcting homework, and meeting with students.

Steve Powell in Portland has firmly refused to let the waves of parental emails overwhelm him and his teachers. He asks parents to contact teachers during office hours, posted in the school's newsletter. "Our primary job is to interact with children. We are not going to answer emails during our teaching day." Powell himself answers parent emails in a timely fashion, but he doesn't feel compelled to answer immediately. Some educators do see advantages to email. Carol Blejwas, who teaches a standard level history course to ninth graders at Hall High School, credits email with providing a new point of entry for parents, who might not have gotten involved in their kids' education in the past. For example, some moms and dads of her ninth graders speak English as a second language, and email makes it easier for them to communicate. This year, for example, she had ten parents show up for conferences, as opposed to one parent the year before.

The patterns of communication among students, parents, and educators in the years before college, and the dependent behaviors they foster, often continue into the college years. Without a history of heavy involvement in the child's earlier years, parents aren't likely to edit their kids' papers in college or intervene in roommate disputes or argue with a professor about a grade. Our survey research shows that the more parents did this kind of thing in high school, the more likely they are to continue it into college, and the less happy their kid is likely to be, both with school and with her relationship with her parents.

This means that learning to back off in high school, gradually surrendering control to the child, is really important. Stop and think the next time you want to intervene. You may want to ask yourself whose needs you are really serving. Certainly you might feel good by solving his problem, but are you really helping your child in the long run? Some parents equate being helpful in this way with being a good parent and derive a lot of satisfaction and identity from that. But parents need to taper off their involvement as their child grows.

On a practical level, you might ask yourself: Is there another way this problem can be solved? Is there a reason I think I need to be the one to solve it? How can I empower my child to take more responsibility?

Imagine that your child is writing a school paper and asks you to proofread it, and you find that it is both badly researched and poorly written. If you rewrite it yourself you have rescued a kid who will expect you to continue to bail him out and whose skills remain poor. Consider a conversation that begins, "How do you feel about the work you've done here so far? What else do you think you need to do to improve it?" You might help guide your child through the process if that's needed, but beware of doing the work for him.

Similarly, when your child comes home and tells you that she blew an exam and it's the teacher's fault because he didn't explain what they should study and the test included material she didn't expect to be there, beware of an impulse to contact the teacher or principal. Open a line of inquiry and try reflecting back what might be going on: "Are you upset you didn't do as well as you hoped?" Sometimes kids learn to externalize blame, when they need to take responsibility for their own actions and improve their own behavior. Supporting them in their blame of others doesn't help them in that regard. And sometimes they just need to accept that they can't control everything—nor can their parents.

## More Anxiety: The Illusion of Instant Contact

Parents and kids often view cell phones as an extension of the parents' ability to protect their kids, no matter how old their kids are. But things happen. Batteries run out; cell phones get lost; adults and kids forget to turn them on or leave their ringer on silent, or they don't answer them. Because we are conditioned to expect an immediate response and consider cell phones as a way to stay safe, we worry that something may have gone wrong. The illusion of instant accessibility and security actually ramps up parents' anxiety. This anxiety in varying degrees is shared by parents of kids with cell phones who are old enough to have some measure of independence in middle or high school.

One family therapist, who didn't want us to use her name, found herself in the same position as many of her anxious clients. One Saturday she left early in the morning for an emergency session with a patient, knowing that her son, a junior in high school, was planning to study as he always did at the library of a nearby university. "I didn't see him that morning because of an emergency session, and then I didn't hear from him until six p.m. I texted him before that and said, 'Please call home.'" She wasn't tremendously worried; the library was in a safe neighborhood and the weather was good. Still, she had this small doubt, fueled by this feeling: "You need to keep in touch. We have this sort of idea that if you can keep in touch, you should."

While her concern was on the mild side, parents whose child is on a college campus, away from home, can feel real anxiety when they don't have the contact that they planned to have. The unpopularity of landlines, with the younger generation especially (and their removal from many dorm rooms), means that parents may have *only* the cell phone as a means of access. There's no waiting roommate who might take the call instead or who might listen to the answering machine even if your kid doesn't. Many parents feel growing unease when they can't reach their kid as quickly as expected. Some overly anxious parents try too hard to stay connected to their kids, hoping that frequent calls and text messages somehow will keep them safe, a tactic that often backfires. A study by a California State University professor found that the teenagers who were most frequently called by their parents were less honest with them.

Developing a regular check-in time can be helpful, as well as learning to get comfortable without constant updates. One mom described her realization that the anxiety was her own problem and that she had to address it herself. She recognized that it had begun to impair her relationship with her daughter and had gotten out of control. Her daughter was adventurous and planning a semester abroad, and the mom knew this was the time to tame her own anxiety, given how much her daughter would be out of her control at that point. She knew that she didn't want to hold her daughter back.

Parents need to learn early on how to recognize when they are overly anxious about their child's behaviors and to beware of getting drawn into a culture of fear and worry. Parent Lenore Skenazy captures this well in the title of her book *Free-Range Kids: Giving Our Children the Freedom We Had without Going Nuts with Worry*. She dispels the myths of the current anxieties of modern parenting and suggests that parents lighten up and give their kids room to grow more freely, without constant parental intervention that borders on the neurotic. We echo her advice: "Quit trying to control everything. It doesn't work anyway." Allow children room to play, to make mistakes, to explore at least some of the world on their own. If it's your own anxiety that stops this from happening, consider what your fears are, identify whether they are valid or worth the worry, and address them.

*Cell Phones as Safety Net: False Security*
An ad by T Mobile illustrates the trend of parents trying to make sure their children are safe by staying in continual touch or always being available. A happy young mom jogs, cell phone in hand. "I take my family everywhere I run," the ad says. "I hear from them at least once a mile." It appears that mom needs to have a strong cell phone signal in the event that she gets "a crisis call about a missing binkie." While the ad makes light of a young mother's hypervigilance and our involved parent culture, its more serious subtext is that moms and dads feel the need to be constantly accessible and that they are expected to be concerned with their children's safety no matter how far away they are.

This need to be on call can generate a lot of tension for conscientious parents. When they realize how much their kids depend on this instant access, many become even more stressed, a pattern Abby found in her reporting. The experience of one family from Philadelphia vividly makes this point. The daughter, a high school junior, was enjoying a later curfew and greater independence in choosing her classes and afterschool activities. Her parents suspected she might be flirting with typical adolescent risks. They gave as much guidance as they could while still trying to nurture her growing ability to manage her own life. In the end they knew that *she* would make those choices, not they. But one morning at breakfast she surprised them. Both parents had accidentally left their cell phones off the night before and their daughter was upset because she had tried unsuccessfully to reach them. "You know, Mom, I really can be comfortable with this new freedom that I have and the responsibility that I have if I know that I can get a hold of you. When I have my cell phone in my pocket, that's like having you there, and if something bad happens, then I can reach you."

The parents were stunned, never imagining that their daughter relied so much on having instant access to them. "Her sense of risk taking is tied to me being the safety net," her mother said. "I don't ever really remember my parents being a safety net." They also felt a little guilty for not being available. Both parents are vigilant now about keeping their cell phones always charged, always on, because their daughter might need them.

Four out of five teens in a survey by the wireless telecommunications industry (CTIA-The Wireless Association) and Harris Interactive said their cell phones made them feel safe. Cell phones can create a sense of false security, however, possibly prompting adolescents to increase their risk taking, believing the phone will serve as a safety net. Make sure that your child does not think of the cell phone as a lifeline. Discuss genuine risks and strategies of avoidance, not just plans for rescue. With teens these conversations can include how to handle offers of drugs and alcohol, avoiding unwanted sexual activity, and which areas in your community are safe and which are not.

In Barbara's survey parents in frequent contact with their college-age sons and daughters expressed concern over the consequences of being so instantly available. "It was easier [when I went to college] to make your own mistakes and learn from them because of the lack of instant communication," wrote one parent. College deans share these worries, saying that many students today don't take the time to contemplate their sometimes reckless behavior nor accept its consequences. Instead they just speed-dial mom or dad to get them out of a jam.

## Advice for Parents

A whirl of cultural and personal forces have brought parents to this point, not least among them unquestioning love and commitment to their kids. From the moment children arrive, parents are bombarded with messages to stay involved from cradle to college, and in the years after that. The belief that staying engaged will protect kids from all kinds of evils and will help get them into college is now a parenting mantra. Our culture's affinity for involved parenting and our ability to communicate so readily enables parents to stay connected to their kids in ways unimaginable a generation ago. But parents may be paying a price for this cultural and wireless bond, far greater than the cost of a rollover or extra-minutes plan.

The ideal situation is to stay involved in your children's life, but not to the extent that you live too much in their life and not enough in your own. Be available, but not so constantly that you feel anxious, stressed, and guilty when you don't respond immediately to your child's text or call. Realize that cell phones are not a safety net, as much as we all might like them to be. Teach your children not to count on their cell phone as a way to save themselves from risky behaviors.

In your efforts to help your kids you may be afraid to let them fail or be unhappy temporarily, even in schools and homes that are characterized by compassion. Remember that children learn from their mistakes, coupled with loving guidance. We suspect that some parents' motivation to prevent their child from making mistakes comes from the substantial pressure to get into college. Try to resist that pressure and that of your peers to overmanage your children's academic life and other activities. Remember, they are the ones going to college, not you (even though you may be paying for it), and they need to own this experience to get the most from it.

The patterns of involvement and communication that you establish in your child's early years will carry over into college. If you respect your child's privacy, listen without judgment, and offer advice when asked, the rewards will lie both in your child's development as well as in the relationship between you and your child.

We close this chapter with a story about Buck's mom, who seems to have figured out how to do this. She has sent her three boys off to college, and each time her heart ached. But as she learned in their high school years, they need to have some space and experience college on their own. Unlike many of her friends, when her sons were in high school she didn't chaperone their dances unless they wanted her there. And most times, they didn't. In college she has tried to practice the same thoughtful parenting, even though she misses them. She doesn't constantly call them or pick their majors. She and her husband are helpful in ways that their sons appreciate. For example, when each boy moved to a new apartment, she and her husband helped set up his new digs, lugging a vat of barbecue or their signature white chili. They wouldn't leave the apartment until there were clean sheets on the bed.

When she calls her kids, she calls at night, when they are out of class or work. A good part of the time she lets them call her. Buck regularly calls as he walks between classes, and so do his brothers. They often ask about their parents' life. "I tried very hard not to be a helicopter parent," she said. "I have to hold myself back from calling. I will send a little email if there's been a breakup with a girlfriend or they have been sick. I don't want to smother them." If she's worried and calls about a sensitive topic, they have the kind of relationship where they will be honest and say they don't want to talk then. "I'll say, 'Call me back when you do.'" And many times they do call back. By practicing restraint and listening to her kids' cues, she and her husband have achieved a warm, loving relationship with their nearly adult children, a constant source of joy.

## Chapter 7

# Moms and Dads, Sons and Daughters

## Styles of Communicating

An upperclassman at a large Midwestern university, Stacey is in constant touch with her mom through Facebook, the uber–social networking site. Mom uses it to keep an eye on Stacey's campus life. Stacey's cell phone is linked to Facebook, and throughout the day she receives a stream of comments from mom about the photos on Stacey's Facebook page or the messages that her friends write there. Stacey always answers her mom, who is waiting, hundreds of miles away in a southern state, for her daughter's immediate response. Stacey spends up to an hour a day responding to her mom, which sometimes is a pain because Stacey is enrolled in the university's most prestigious school and is very busy. In addition she and her mom text a lot and talk on the phone at least once a week, and Skype too.

Stacey and her mom are not all that unusual. Our surveys found that nearly three-quarters of female students talk to mom more than dad, and that's in every conceivable way: calling, texting, on Skype, emailing, even sending the occasional card. Our reporting also shows a lot of contact between daughters and moms on Facebook, just like Stacey and her mother. That fits with psychological research that the mother-daughter relationship is typically the strongest in the family.

But there's another profound bond at work here—her feelings for dad. "I wish that I had more communication with dad," Stacey says. "I miss him more than the rest of my family sometimes." She says she is just as close to her dad but is in less contact with him. That's something she's not happy about.

Many students are in the same boat as Stacey. While the majority of survey students were satisfied with how much they talked to mom, 33 percent of daughters and 17 percent of sons wanted more conversation with dad. Abby's independent interviews with students at other colleges suggest that the number of students wanting a greater connection with dad may be even higher. Given the opportunity during interviews to reflect and talk about their relationships with their dad, most students said they wanted more contact with him than they currently have, even if initially they had said they were fine with their present level of contact.

Most parents have cell phones and most college students are glued to their cell phones or laptops. So if they want to talk to dad more often, why aren't they texting him, or tapping out a quick email? On the other hand, why isn't dad punching in a speed-dial or two? And then, of course, the biggest question is: How much should they be talking to mom and dad anyway?

The answers aren't so simple. As most families can attest, moms and dads and daughters and sons communicate differently. These patterns are well-documented by psychologists, and our survey results support them. Girls have been socialized to talk more, and boys to talk less. "In most cases parents tend to talk more to their girls, and they tend to play more with their sons," said Dr. Kathleen Galvin, who teaches about family communication at Northwestern

135

University. "This is setting the pattern. Both parents still talk more to daughters than they do their sons across all age levels. Mothers also talk more to their children than fathers do." These patterns may change, though, because today's younger parents are more likely to share in child rearing, she added.

Our data show that daughters connect with their parents more often than sons do, at the rate of 14.5 compared to 11.3 times per week. To most parents, especially parents of teenage girls, it's a no-brainer that daughters are talking more than sons, although it might be surprising just how much the sons are communicating. Moms initiate more contact than dads do, which also isn't surprising, but these numbers barely hint at the larger story.

Cell phones and computers have revolutionized our way of life, and now they are transforming how family members relate to each other. The growth of single-parent and blended families, combined with the evolution of moms in the workforce and dads in the soccer carpool, are pushing this change too. Kids now call, text, or email whichever parent is more available. Forget about calling the land-line at home or the office; a parent might be busy or not pick up right away. "I can't stand voicemail. It tears at my soul!" explains Ben, a Boston University student. His buddies gathered around him in the university's commons agree. Today many kids want an immediate response, and some adults do too. It is also the case, of course, that sometimes they don't want that immediate connection and opt for texting or emailing, just as adults do, when a fast response isn't expected or when it just seems more comfortable or a better fit with the message.

The opportunity to communicate around-the-clock from texting to Facebook, fueled by our cultural expectation for immediate contact, can stress the normal bonds in any parent-child combination. Regardless of a child's sex, too much contact with parents hobbles students who are trying to reach adulthood. And when children call each parent directly, they may reduce contact with the parent to whom they aren't so close. At least in the past, when a student called home on the landline, that parent might have gotten a minute or two of air time.

On the upside, this trend is creating fresh opportunities for parents and children to draw closer. Sometimes mom's not available when a burning question arises on campus, and so dad gets the call. Understanding these changing family dynamics is vital for parents and students who want to improve their relationships during the college years and beyond.

## Why Kids Talk More to Mom

Dr. Linda Nielsen, a professor of educational and adolescent psychology at Wake Forest University, has thought a lot about students like Stacey and their desire to talk more with their dads. She has taught about father-daughter relationships at the college level for the past twenty years and authored books on the subject, including *Between Fathers & Daughters* and *Embracing Your Father: Creating the Relationship You Want with Your Dad.* "The mother is communication central for the family. You can't communicate with the family without going through mom," she said during an interview. "What we've got here is a culture that believes the typical way an average family should communicate is through mom. This is considered normal, whether it's Facebooking, Twittering, emailing, or phoning." Nielsen and other experts believe that our culture has socialized all of us to regard mom as the family's communications hub. Nielsen also believes that mom is not being intentionally "mean" to dad by controlling so much communication: "She's simply acting out the societal script that we trained her for forty years to act out."

## Why That's Changing

Written when *Leave It to Beaver* ruled, the script that mothers control family communication is now showing its age. In the 1950s and 1960s dad was typically the breadwinner, too busy for the day-to-day details of raising kids. Mom was most likely at home with the children, always ready with a sympathetic ear or shoulder. Generations have been socialized to view mothers as big-hearted caregivers and fathers as less emotionally engaged.

Today, however, more moms work outside the home; many earn more than their husbands. A divorce rate of 50 percent creates more single-parent and blended families than in the past. Still, mom's availability for nurturing is aided by cell phones and also lengthened by adult children's trend of marrying later. Without the competing presence of a spouse, young adults have more time and emotional energy for mom.

## Dads Are Becoming More Involved

Many dads are now taking on a bigger role in raising kids, and more dads are staying at home, although not nearly as much as mothers. Increasingly those dads who work outside the home are pitching in on child care, joining PTAs, and schlepping kids to school and other activities in the family van (or as Abby's son Jack calls it when his dad is at the wheel, the "man-van").

Compared to forty years ago, today's dads are much more involved with their children. A 2006 University of Maryland study of married men from 1965 to 2000 showed a dramatic, 153 percent increase in the time dads spent playing, feeding, bathing, and otherwise caring for their kids, from 2.6 to 6.5 hours per week. Dr. Melissa A. Milkie, one of the study's lead authors and a professor of social psychology at the university, says two factors account for the change: "One, there's been a real cultural shift toward more involved fathering. It's not only okay, it's seen as a very positive thing. And, two, there's been a real structural pull for fathers to be home because their wives are out earning money."

Dad's increase in child rearing has led to deeper relationships with his kids. "I'm just finding more young men who are feeling very close to their fathers than in years past. The level of communication has opened up between fathers and sons that didn't exist in past generations," observes Dr. Michael J. Diamond, a psychologist and expert on fatherhood. Author of *My Father Before Me: How Fathers and Sons Influence Each Other throughout Their Lives* and the father of two 20-somethings, Diamond has spent much of his professional life studying fathers.

In fact Diamond said that if our survey had been taken twenty years ago, he believes 50 percent of the sons would have wanted more contact with dad, not the 17 percent we found. He expressed surprise that 33 percent of daughters wanted more contact, expecting the number to be higher. As girls sexually mature they typically need to figure out how to relate as a young woman to their dad. Boyfriends, dating, and sex are now part of their lives, and young women have traditionally been uncomfortable talking about these topics with parents, especially their dad. This awkwardness is part of our culture, and it marks the often poignant change in the relationship between fathers and daughters. When daughters are young, dads are able to express their affection easily, with hugs, piggyback rides, and other physical displays. But that changes as daughters develop sexually and dads become unsure of how to relate to them. Sadly, but understandably, dads can become distant. The easy, affectionate gestures that once characterized their relationship with their daughter are now bestowed with caution. Given this rocky phase of doubt, separation, and redrawing of the relationship, one might expect even more daughters to express a longing for increased communication with dad, or at least the relationship they used to have before sex and dating appeared on the horizon.

Dad's role is changing, but not in every family, nor at the same pace. At Northwestern, Kathleen Galvin sees evidence of a gradual shift in her class discussions: "Now I have a number of students who have stay-at-home dads and the reverse is true for them. They say, 'I am much closer to my dad than my mom.' I think certainly it will be a long time before a dramatic shift occurs in a very large number of households, but clearly there are some households where this shift is occurring."

### Some Dads Have Catching Up to Do

The shift hasn't reached the family of Patty, a student at a small, private school who describes her southern family as conventional; her interactions with her dad reflect that. "If I call home with a problem, I will ask to speak to mom. Rarely do I call and say, 'Put dad on the phone.' He has a fix-it mentality. He's very direct, whereas my mother will entertain my words. My dad will be, like, 'Let's get to the point.' I think dad is socialized that way, but I know he would do anything for me."

Jodi, an upperclassman at a large public university, is part of the same culture as Patty. A self-described "daddy's girl," Jodi talks daily to her mom and, typically once every week or so, to her dad. She says she talks more to mom because her father works long hours. "Dads are working. Dads are supporting the family. If he doesn't call, don't complain," she says in a phone interview. "That's why I haven't said anything. I think that's why it's not really upsetting to me, but I would like it if he called." She pauses while she contemplates why he fails to phone. "I don't know the psyche of a fifty-year-old man. I wonder why he doesn't. Is it because he's so tired? After work he has to do bills and yard work. I think he doesn't know that he can call." On the rare occasions when Jodi calls home and dad answers because her mom is unavailable, he assumes that she just wants to talk to mom. "We use mom to talk through," she says.

Many dads might actually want more conversation but have been habitually relegated to a brief hello. It may help dads to know that many college students want more contact with them, and that developing this rapport is well worth the effort. Some tips for dads: If this is new to you and you don't want to talk long, do what students do and call during any situation that makes the call finite. Try it while you're walking the dog. Ask open-ended questions about how the week has been or about school, such as "What's your favorite class this semester?" Tell stories about what's gone on at home or at work. Let them know you care.

---

Please don't text or call while driving, given the known dangers.

---

## Why Guys Talk Less

Jodi's voice is pitch perfect, according to Galvin. In her class she asks students what happens when they call home. "If dad picks up the phone, they'll say, 'Dad says a couple of things and then he hands the phone to mom and says mom will catch me up.' It's as if dad doesn't know how to hold that conversation," Galvin said. "Sometimes a female student will call dad at work to force a conversation."

Sometimes, as other students told us, they have conversations with dad only when they are actually doing something "random" with him, like buying a grill or driving together in the car. Men are socialized as boys in this kind of behavior; they make friends by playing rather than talking. Because parents generally have talked less to their sons than to their daughters, the result is that, on average, guys talk less than girls. This fact especially resonates with Jack, a North Carolina State University student, who has three sisters. "Me and my dad would go watch football and my mom and my sisters would talk constantly. They were talking to each other, talking on the phone, and then they would have sleepovers, with even more talking." Jack, though, thinks all that gabbing has rubbed off on him in a positive way. Now he talks more than many of his male friends. "I'm a very social type of person," he says, and that has made life easier for him.

Having been brought up to be less talkative, dads are now learning to communicate more with their kids, but there's a learning curve. Getting calls from children who demand an immediate response can be annoying at times, especially to parents who aren't used to it. Because of Abby's schedule, she always has been more available to handle emergency calls from her two sons and is more accustomed to it, not that she especially likes it. For example, Abby's son Jack called her because his high school didn't have his emergency contact form on file and he wouldn't be allowed to attend classes that day unless a parent came to sign it. (For the record, Abby did go to school to sign the form, as did a bunch of other parents.) Abby's husband, J.D., an attorney, hasn't always gotten as many calls from their sons. But that has been changing since he and Jack got cell phones. Now J.D. is also on the receiving end of calls from Jack and his younger brother Carlos about car problems and missing soccer shin guards. "You have to pick up because you don't know if it's serious or not," says J.D. The calls have often interrupted work conference calls, and J.D., involved father though he is, admits to being a little irritated. Talk with your kids in advance about when it's okay to call at work on the cell phone and what constitutes an emergency. Suggest that if they just want to talk or ask a nonurgent question during work hours, they can start with a text message, such as "Hi, are you available? Just want to talk, nothing urgent."

## Mom's New Roles

Some moms may have a hard time giving up their role as the family's communication center. At least when it comes to moms talking to their daughters, part of this reluctance may stem from the profound bond between mother and daughter, including the latest variation on this bond, mom as daughter's best friend, which students Molly and Rebecca described. "It's actually a generational reality," said Galvin. "Many students will talk to parents three to five times per day and usually they are talking to mom." This super bond between mother and daughter may also help explain another of our survey findings: sons (37 percent) are more likely than daughters (20 percent) to talk equally with both parents.

This new closeness also may reinforce mom's traditional role as the chief communicator. As Stacey and other students told us, when they call home mom dominates. "Mom doesn't want to give the phone to dad," says Stacey. "She'll say he's too busy." Without prompting, Stacey offers, "If we're on the phone with dad, she fears [that we'll hang up] and she won't hear from us for a while." Stacey also hints at another reason: information is power. "The women in our family are hogs. They like to know things in the family before the men in the family do." Although this is certainly not true for all moms, Stacey raises some interesting and provocative points. Women have been socialized to have certain expectations, and when they no longer meet them or their role changes, they may have trouble adjusting. As Galvin says, "It's hard not being the mom that you expected to be and having a husband or partner who is very good at some of this with the kids. Mom is the person everyone talked to, and you took status and satisfaction from that role."

As the number of dual-career couples increases, this notion of mom as the family dispatcher is losing traction. Many moms want and even insist on their husband's increased involvement with their children. Wives try to foster their husband's participation because it benefits the children as well as the men, and it relieves women from the constant demand of raising their kids. But sometimes old cultural patterns get in the way, and some students view their mother's and father's roles differently and expect less of dad. "My mom is sometimes critical of dad and says that he needs to do more parenting," said Marilyn, a student at a large public university, whose mom doesn't work outside the home. "But I feel he works and makes all the money and she should carry more weight around the house."

## Moms on Facebook

Sometimes moms take their role as communications central a little too far—and it's easy to go too far when armed with a cell phone, a computer, and the notion that a parent can be her child's best friend. The stress of a life altered by an empty, or nearly empty, nest can push a parent overboard. As they see their children move away, some parents hang on as tightly as they can. In some cases, like Stacey's, it would appear that mom may be playing the maternal card a little too much if she expects her daughter to spend an hour a day responding to her questions about photos and comments on Facebook.

Stacey is sympathetic to her mother's desire for closeness. She understands how radically life changed for her mom since she left for college and her older sister got married. When they were younger, Stacey's mother would talk to them every day after school. She wanted to know it all, what happened in each class, details about fights with friends, and how they really felt each day when they walked in the door. Sometimes it was just too much.

Still, observes Stacey, she nurtured and supported them as best she could and, in the process, gained a deep understanding of her daughters and their lives. "Now she can't do that anymore. Now she has to rely on us to tell her," says Stacey. That is, except when she goes on Facebook. "She can go through our photos and [friends' comments] and pick up different things about our lives." When Stacey went to college and mom signed up for Facebook, Stacey was reluctant to "friend" her (give permission to access her Facebook page). "It was an invasion of privacy, and I had thought that I had gotten away from that when I moved away from home," she said. But with college so new and challenging, Stacey relented, admitting, "At the same time, it is kind of comforting."

Sometimes Stacey regrets her decision. "She's kind of a Facebook stalker," she said. On occasion friends write on Stacey's wall, telling her to have a better week or asking why she didn't attend a certain event. The subtext, of course, is that Stacey had some kind of problem that week. Then mom pounces, immediately calling or messaging her daughter to find out what's going on. So does Stacey's grandmother, who is also on Facebook. "She is even creepier than my mom," Stacey said.

Other students said they friended their moms more out of a sense of obedience than anything else. "Most people don't want to friend their parents, and if they do, they do it because they have to," says Britney, a 20-year-old sophomore who friended her mom. "My mom has never known her age. She tries to be cool with the kids." Other students allow their mother access because they don't want to incur her anger.

Some moms have a much lower profile with their children. Marie has three children; one is a student at Northeastern University, and the others are in high school. All are on Facebook, and she hasn't asked them to friend her. "I've always fought this culture of parental intervention. There's something about it that I don't like," she said over coffee in a café in the affluent Connecticut town of Avon. "I've tried to step back a little and not be in teachers' faces and let things unfold. On the other hand, I'm not 'hands-off' like my parents were." Encouraging her children to have experiences separate from the family is important to Marie. When the kids were younger they went to sleepaway camp for several weeks each summer. Spending time away with new friends and different activities helped them build a stronger identity and become more independent, she says. Though not exactly a summer camp, Facebook is a communal experience that serves some of those same purposes for teens and college students. Even so, Marie admits to occasionally checking out her younger children's Facebook pages when they inadvertently leave their laptops open.

Many moms are on Facebook, busy creating social networks of their own but in some cases also monitoring their kids' pages. The issue of moms using Facebook to track their kids' lives is now rich material for websites, commercials, and parodies. In 2009 the Onion, an Internet-based, satirical "news service," created a hilarious segment on the trend: "Facebook, Twitter Revolutionizing How Parents Stalk Their College-Age Kids." The clip features two news anchors and an aging soccer-mom type, dubbed "E-Mom," who advises parents how to track their grown children's personal lives through Facebook and Twitter. "I look through all of my son Jeffrey's photos every single day," says E-Mom, showing a photo of her son with a young woman, her curves bursting out of a skimpy top. By using a Facebook feature called "tagging," E-Mom shows parents how to identify the people in photos posted on their child's page. E-Mom goes on to tell parents how to surreptitiously monitor their kids' every movement by getting on Twitter, an Internet-based service that allows members to send out brief messages (tweets) that can be read by anyone who signs on. Gushes E-Mom, "You can hear their every thought. It's like a dream come true!" The story concludes with the reporter commenting, "Now the only excuse for not knowing every detail of your child's life is having a life of your own."

A mother's bond with her children is powerful, and once they go off to college it's often heart-wrenching for her. It is understandable that, in this age of instant communication, a mom can overdo it Facebooking, calling, and texting her kids. But in order to help her children grow up she needs to give them room, which she can't do when she's scouring her children's Facebook pages.

## Social Media: A Quick Guide

Most college students have an account on Facebook, a social networking site. Once open only to college students, now anyone over 13 can join. (Some have accounts on MySpace, which operates similarly but is less commonly used by college students; it is popular, however, for its musical offerings.) Each person has a home page, where they receive an ongoing newsfeed from their friends, including status updates, photos, and links to websites, videos, or news stories. Users post their own updates to a page called a "wall"; these updates, in turn, show up on their friends' newsfeeds. Updates typically describe what someone is doing or thinking or wants to comment on and can be updated as often as desired. Friends can also write on a user's wall by leaving comments or notes or birthday wishes or by clicking a button that they "like" something already posted. In addition, users have a "profile" with a photo and whatever general description they wish to provide about themselves, including contact information, education and work background, and personal preferences, such as religious and political views, musical tastes, and favorite books, movies, and television shows. Each user can decide how much of his information is available for anyone to see and how much of it is shared with friends only (or with other select groups, such as a work or school network). Another link takes the viewer to a page that aggregates all the users' photos. Friends can "tag" each other in photos as well, so if someone takes a picture at a party and then clicks on a face in the photo and inserts the name of the person, that friend has been "tagged" and will receive an email alert. Facebook also has its own message system and chat function.

Anyone with a Facebook account can search for potential friends, either by name or by searching networks such as a high school or college graduating class. They simply find the person in the directory and click to send a request to "friend" the individual, who then receives an email asking him to "confirm" or "ignore" the request. "Unfriending"—the process by which a user discontinues a Facebook friend's access to his page, perhaps after a falling out—is another Facebook term. It was named the 2009 "word of the year" by the New Oxford American Dictionary.

Twitter is another social networking tool that allows users to send short bursts of text (up to 140 characters) to all their "followers." These status updates are called "tweets." These brief messages are often as simple as a quick announcement of where the person is going to be ("Headed to Irish Pub to watch Arsenal soccer match") or a pithy statement ("Yes, it's raining here, AGAIN") or an inquiry of followers ("Know a good place to get a haircut on the South Side?"), with answers promptly tweeted back. Twitter followers often post quite frequently, and young professionals especially use it for networking and information exchange. The Twitter profile of a user shows the number of people being followed and the number of people following that person. Becoming a follower is as simple as clicking on a box that says, "follow that person"; this triggers a notification to the person being followed.

## Dads on Facebook

Fathers also have joined Facebook, but industry statistics suggest that their numbers are substantially lower than the moms'. Some dads are engaging in the same kind of tactics as Stacey's mom, however. A student columnist at Binghamton University recently wrote about her loss of privacy when her dad pressured her to friend him on Facebook. Other dads take a much lower-key approach. One dad asked his three college-age daughters if they were agreeable to his joining Facebook because of his job. "It's up to you if you want to be my friend or not," he said. His daughters all friended him, even the one who tended to push the envelope partying and smoking. "I don't go searching through their Facebook files and I don't spend a lot of time on Facebook with them. It's a supplemental form of communication," he said. Some dads avoid Facebook because their wives are on it. Britney's father won't join Facebook. She says, "He doesn't want to be that annoying dad on Facebook and he kind of knows my mom is one of those moms on Facebook."

Other dads use it to monitor behavior just as moms do. A junior in Barbara's course on adolescent development forwarded an email from her dad, admonishing her about what she described as "a curse word in my current status [update]," ostensibly to protect her mother. The student said she was "both amused and offended by his email." Her reaction? "I unfriended him."

Parents on Facebook invariably evoke both giggles and sighs. E-MOM, the Internet caricature, resonates wildly with college kids and social pundits. But she's not that far removed from any number of well-intentioned parents trying to remain connected and keep their kids safe in the unknown world of college. Despite their parents' generally positive motives, many students tend to view them much like bothersome relatives who overstay their welcome: people they have to put up with because they are, after all, family. Of course some students have found a way to get around this intrusion. They create a second Facebook page or adjust the privacy settings on their first page, blocking their parents' (and grandparents') access. Facebook demographics and the need for parental oversight continue to evolve, as middle school students are now joining. However, parents would be wise to allow their college-age children to have some independence on the site.

149

## How Kids Relate to Each Parent

Typically sons and daughters discuss different topics with their parents. For example, our survey research shows that sons are more likely than daughters to talk to their dads about casual dating, serious relationships, parties, and their sex life. Daughters, on the other hand, are more likely to discuss these topics with their moms.

Sex is not something daughters easily discuss with their fathers, and fathers may talk around the subject, warning daughters of what young men want but rarely discussing the details of having sex. Michael Diamond points out, "It's a difficult age. You can't talk about sex with dad, and it's a period where sexuality is important. It's a lot easier for boys to talk about sex with their father than for girls to talk about it. Even if a boy is recounting conquests, he can do it in a light way with dad, but a daughter doesn't do that."

When Jodi, a student at a large public university, had a pregnancy scare, she couldn't tell her dad, but she could tell her mom, calling her the morning after she slept with her date, explaining that the condom had ruptured. Jodi says she is very open and proud about her sex life, but she couldn't imagine telling her dad about it.

Some fathers and daughters do have those conversations. One father, who was divorced when his three daughters were on the verge of adolescence, was determined to stay a big part of their lives. An administrator at a large university, he used all the communication skills he had acquired working with college students, including a good dash of humor, to have a running conversation over the years with his daughters about sensitive subjects such as alcohol, drugs, and sex. When the young women became sexually active in their college years, one Valentine's Day he gave them each condoms. His efforts to create candor about these taboo topics have been successful, and now his daughters initiate these delicate conversations with him.

## The Mother-Son Connection

Many male students enjoy a very close relationship with their moms. Several jokingly referred to themselves as a member of the "Mama's Boy Club." Sons have traditionally sought out mom when they need a little nurturing, and many moms feel fulfilled when they can provide that care, especially to a son in college who has one foot already out the door. Michael Diamond also sees this type of interaction among his patients. "A lot say they talk to mother about mothering types of things. One boy said he likes to talk to his mother because she can be a caretaker. He calls her when his back hurts or he has a cold. He knows his mother loves to be in the motherly caretaking roles. Another kid said, 'Mom is more empathetic and she can put herself in my shoes.' Dad, on the other hand, is a tough-love kind of guy."

In years past "mama's boy" was shorthand for a son so tied to his mom that he was unable to act independently, but we found that students with these close relationships prided themselves on being independent. Marcus, a senior at the University of Minnesota, has worked his way through college, paying his own bills, doing his own laundry, and writing his own papers. But he has a deep respect and affection for his mother and stays in close contact with her. Marcus is unabashed about answering his mother's calls in front of his friends. In fact he says, "I wouldn't want to be friends with anyone if I didn't feel comfortable talking [to my mom] in front of them."

Some hundreds of miles southeast of Minnesota, Jamie and Christopher, twin brothers and students at North Carolina State University, share some of Marcus's feelings. Sporting John Deere baseball caps with the slogan "No Farm, No Food," the twins are from a four-generation family farm and are pursuing two-year agricultural science degrees. In the years before college they would rise every day at 5:30 to feed the calves before going to school; after school it was more of the same. Dairy farming is hard, sometimes dangerous work. "We

151

end up saving each other's lives about once a week," says Christopher. They laugh out loud at the thought of parents making wake-up calls to their college students, who otherwise might not make it to class. Their work helps support the family and the next weekend they are going home to help out on the farm. The brothers wouldn't think of refusing their mom's twice-daily calls. "I ain't ashamed of my mama!" Christopher says, and his twin nods in agreement.

Of course this kind of relationship can be intensified with a son or daughter if mom is also a single parent. Levon is a student at North Carolina State University, the oldest child in a family headed by a single mom. He and his mom are extremely close, and the move to college has been hard on both of them. "I don't want to talk about how it used to be," he says, escaping a sweltering August afternoon in the cool of the school's air-conditioned Taco Bell. "She is like my best friend," he says in front of a tableful of friends. He will always answer his mother's call. The same goes for Carlos, a first-generation student at Texas State University. "My goal now is to finish college as fast as I can," he said. With a college degree Carlos plans to move back home to Austin and help support his mother and sister, much as he did in high school when he worked a forty-hour week while attending high school. His mother cleans office buildings, and Carlos, who has a work-study job at college, is determined to help her. It does not occur to him to ignore his mother's calls. "Not answering? That's weird," he said. "I find that funny." He says that it is part of his Mexican American culture to respect his mom. "You talk back to your mom and your grandma will hit you. You need to respect mom."

Several factors seem to influence this kind of intense mother-son and mother-daughter relationship, and one may be ethnicity. Dr. Barbara Penington, a researcher and chair of the Department of Communication at the University of Wisconsin-Whitewater, believes ethnicity does play a part. In a 2001 study she found that, overall, African American daughters were more respectful to their mothers than their white counterparts and argued with their mothers less. That research also has made Penington more observant in her classes with students of color and how they say they interact with their mothers. "I know that from my experience teaching here that African American male students appear very respectful of mothers. The parent, especially the mother, is always the authority." In her class Penington often plays an excerpt of a tape in which an African American mom is very blunt with her daughter about getting poor grades. "The European American kids say, 'Oh, how could that daughter take that! I would have yelled back,' and the African American kids say, 'Oh, no, what your mom says you sit and listen to. She's trying to help you, trying to scare you into doing the right thing.' This also shows me that they really respect their moms." Penington also sees this heightened level of respect for mothers from their daughters in the Latina culture.

## How Cell Phones Are Changing Family Relationships

*Daughters and Dads*
John, a busy physician on the West Coast, is not much of a phone person, and he's definitely not on Facebook or tweeting on Twitter. In fact when his daughter first went to college on the East Coast, his wife did most of the talking with her. "My wife picks up the phone first. She'll end up having a fifteen-minute conversation, and then I add my ninety seconds of whatever." But then one morning during his hour-long commute to work he decided to call Melody himself. Maybe it was remembering how he used to wake his kids for school that prompted him, or maybe he just missed her. A couple years later, he's not sure. Now the calls are an important part of his daily routine driving to and from work. They aren't long, a few minutes at most,

153

just enough to say, "What's on for your day?" and "I love you." "I feel better. It gets my day off to a good start," he says. If for some reason they don't connect—once John lost his cell phone—he feels "very bad." John's other daughter is in school close to home, and though he often sees her on the weekends he's added her to his morning call list. As for Melody, she is quite happy with the whole setup: "I really like being able to check in with my dad because I didn't get to check in with him as much in high school. It's nice to know he's thinking of me." Plus, she says, dad's calls are shorter and less inquisitive than mom's. Now she feels just a bit closer to her dad.

Sometimes it's the daughter who changes things with her dad. Veronica was always closer to her mom before heading off to the University of Minnesota. But Veronica's mom works days as a nurse. She monitors patients closely and is often unavailable when Veronica most needs a reassuring connection with home or some practical advice. Because Veronica's dad is in sales, he's more available to take calls. So Veronica began to call her dad about the puzzling minutiae of a college student's life: the fees on her new checking account, driving directions to a nearby mall, her latest test score, and so on. Next she encouraged her father to learn how to text. "If I text him, now he'll call back," she says with a smile. Their conversations developed a give-and-take that Veronica has come to appreciate. "It's 'How's school? How's work? Just checking up!' I think it's helped a lot that we can talk whenever." She credits the cell phone with bringing her closer to her dad.

### Sons and Dads

Before going to college Brendan was closer to his mom. His father was always the quiet disciplinarian and, while Brendan certainly loves him, their relationship (perhaps because he is the youngest of five) was more distant. Once Brendan got to college, several things happened that would transform their relationship. The first was rooming with a student who enjoyed a very close relationship with his dad. His roommate talked to or texted his dad daily, which at first Brendan thought was weird. "But over time, it became a cool thing," he said, as he watched his friend's father support him through a devastating breakup with his girlfriend and the other ups-and-downs of campus life. At the same time Brendan's dad developed a medical condition, forcing him to retire, and Brendan began to call his dad at home. Whether it was the illness or the retirement, something clicked between father and son. Soon Brendan was talking to his dad several times a week. "I would call dad to tell him I just got out of a physics test and I did a good job or to arrange the next visit." The calls weren't long, but they made Brendan feel warm and connected. "I kind of got the vibe that dad was pleasantly surprised."

A year and a half later, when we talked to Brendan again, we found their relationship had deepened. Now when Brendan goes home he pitches in on his dad's carpentry projects, a new pastime for Brendan. They also sail together. Feeling the pressure of preparing to leave college and find a job, Brendan welcomes his father's new nonjudgmental role in his life. "It makes me feel like I have someone who is looking out for me on a different level than a friend or parent trying to guide me all the time. I'm in a relationship with someone on my side without question." Without the convenience of the cell phone Brendan doubts he would have been able to make the same connection with his dad, given his rigorous class and varsity team schedule. We also saw another element fortifying their relationship: his dad's nonjudgmental attitude toward him. Brendan's dad has the right idea. He actively listens and offers solid support.

### Texting to a Better Relationship

Because typically boys have been socialized to talk less than girls, as teens and young adults they may be more comfortable with less chatting, although there are always exceptions to the rule. The brief, episodic nature of texting is comfortable for them, allowing them to stay in touch with home yet remain independent. We have heard numerous stories about sons texting their dads as, miles apart, they watch the same sporting event or share comments about the latest Quentin Tarantino movie.

One mother, whose son is a sophomore at Tufts and not given to a lot of chitchat, hears more from her son via texting than any other means of communication. And for her, "That's all I need. I know he's okay." In fact texting has helped them stay connected and yet given her son the space he seems to want and need. Recently she and her husband sent their son tickets to a Red Sox game. The game was televised, and while it was on they texted their son, letting him think that they could see him in his Green Monster seats: "Who's that babe you're with?" they typed. He immediately shot back his male roommate's name, and they all shared a good laugh.

Of course texting is also a good option for daughters who find it hard to talk with their parents. Alana, a freshman at Indiana State University, has always been less talkative with her mom, especially compared to her older brother. In some ways it's like pulling teeth to get Alana to actually talk about what's going on in her life. "She'll say, 'Mom, do we have to do this right now?'" said her mother. Yet with texting Alana is an open book. "I feel texting is bringing me closer to her. She can't express to me the way my son can. But when her little thumbs get going I know what's going on with her." In fact, her mom said, "[In high school] I had to tell her to stop text-messaging me from school. . . . I knew all the gossip at school."

Texting is an easy, neutral way for parents and kids to stay in touch. Text messages are generally brief and to the point and, as many parents know all too well, can be answered almost anywhere. Texts can let a worried mom know her child is over a bad stomach bug ("Hi, I'm better") or let dad send positive thoughts to his daughter auditioning for a school musical ("Break a leg! Love, Dad").

Text messages usually lack a tone of voice, which can be a problem when you miss some emotional signals. But missing a nagging or whining tone can also be a real boon. (Of course if there are too many texts, that in itself can spell nagging or whining.)

## The Hazards of Continued Nagging

Unfortunately the power to communicate whenever we want encourages an unpleasant habit, nagging, which is familiar to nearly every parent involved in rushing kids to school, doctor's appointments, piano lessons, and baseball practices without end. ("Please, please, get your backpack, music lesson, water bottle, and get into the car, now!") Parents who call college students with constant reminders to apply for internships, write college papers, and clean their room are nagging, and no one likes it, parents included. When Alex, a freshman at a well-known southern university, took a gap year abroad, he was thrilled when his cell phone got poor reception and he didn't have to talk to his mother. Instead they chatted online. "I just wanted to have nine and a half months of unadulterated alone time, frankly. I just feel like especially mom is very nagging and tries to micromanage my life. She's not quite a helicopter mom. I know some friends whose moms are much worse." For his freshman year Alex plans to keep his calls with mom to a minimum, but he is more open to talking with his dad, who tends to keep things on a lighter tone. For example, Alex and his dad often exchange funny emails.

Students say parents need to lighten up a little. Annoyance, anxiety, and disappointment come across a cell phone almost as clearly as they do in person. Brendan, who rekindled his connection with his dad, now has a tense relationship with his mom. Before college he was always closer to her. "Now I feel there's tension when I'm talking to my mother. It's always—how can I put this—always something

157

more that I need to be doing. If I'm writing a paper at the time and caught up in sports [Brendan plays on a varsity team], if I talk to mom about those things, my mom will say, 'What about your résumé and applying for that job?' There's always something else that I should be doing." Now when his mom calls every two weeks or so, he doesn't always answer. "If I'm in the middle of something, if I'm already anxious about school work, I don't want a phone call that will make me more stressed out," he said. Brendan knows his mother is worried about their relationship, but he doesn't quite know how to fix it, and that makes him uncomfortable too. Sometimes it's easier just to avoid her than to confront his conflicted feelings about the situation.

Brendan senses that his mom is upset about being shut out of his life. To restore their healthy relationship, Brendan's mom might encourage him to build his own to-do lists and find other topics of conversation that aren't focused on what she thinks he needs to accomplish.

By the time they reach college, students need to be ready to manage the routine of their daily lives without continual prodding from parents about schoolwork and other obligations. If they fail to hand in a paper on time, don't sign up for housing for the following year, or miss a deadline for an internship application, that's all part of the learning curve. Yes, it's painful to watch kids fail, especially when parents are paying so much for college these days. But it's also painful to let perpetual nagging ruin your relationship with your child.

## Advice for Parents

Traditional parental roles have changed, and many moms and dads today are filling different roles in the family, workplace, and community. The communications revolution is helping to change these roles. Cell phones link individual family members to each other, unlike the old landline in the family home. The universal demand for instant contact is also adding to the mix. College students are more apt to call the parent they can reach quickly—even if it isn't the parent whom they would have called first in the past, which was often mom. This impatience is opening up fresh avenues of connection in families, which can be a good thing. Our survey showed that kids wanted more connection with dad, and our reporting showed that with just a speed-dial, kids are beginning to make that connection.

Now more daughters are calling dads, and sons are too, when dads are more available than moms. For some moms not always being the parent on call is a relief. For others who are used to being the center of communications, it's a bit unsettling and takes some adjusting. For dads, conversing with their kids may take getting used to. As we learned from our commuting physician on the West Coast and our Red Sox fans on the East Coast, it takes only a few minutes to call or text a message of affection. There's also a line between interfering with a child's life on campus and sending a cheery hello. No student welcomes a daily discussion about upcoming papers or a constant stream of nagging calls about job applications and other tasks. College students need space to become independent, and parents need to have respect for their boundaries.

We hope that dads will consider taking more steps to reach out to their college-age children and might see this as a way to build a bond that will last well into adulthood. If texting or emailing is comfortable, use it. The occasional phone call also means a lot to many kids, and it doesn't have to be long or chatty. It can be as simple as "Just thinking about you and wanted to say hi. How are things going?" Moms and daughters have traditionally enjoyed a strong bond. Daughters may have lots of friends, but they have only one mom. Moms can be close to their daughters, but they need to preserve their role as parent. The same advice applies to dads.

## Chapter 8

# Students with Learning Issues and Medical Concerns

A t the orientation for the University of Arizona's acclaimed pro-gram for students with learning and attention challenges, parents and students are split up into different groups, a strategy now common at many colleges to emphasize the soon-to-be separation. That doesn't keep them from talking to each other. "We have parents who haven't been separated for more than an hour and they are already texting their kids," said Dr. Jeff Orgera, director of the university's Strategic Alternative Learning Techniques (SALT) Center. As soon as students are accepted, SALT works mightily to encourage them to take charge of their education, emailing various to-do lists to the students (not their parents). Orgera and his staff also urge families to limit contact with their children to a few scheduled times per week. "But I have to be honest. That doesn't really happen," he said. "After an exam you can hear them calling mom and dad. The exam hasn't even been graded but they are already strategizing on what to do, [whether] to call the professor."

Many parents of students with such challenges are so used to being their child's advocate that it's hard for them to step aside when their children head off to college. It also may be hard for their children, who may depend on mom and dad to do all the strategizing and talking on their behalf. Without their guiding hand, parents may worry about how their children will handle all the stresses and opportunities of life at college while also managing their learning disability. The same goes for parents of students with serious medical conditions. It's difficult enough for parents of students without such challenges as dyslexia or diabetes to maintain a close connection with their kids while encouraging them to be independent; for these parents, it can be even harder.

Consider the experiences of Joanie and her son Tim, who has learning and psychological problems (not a rare combination) and is now in his first year in college. They have a powerful bond, forged by their intense rapport and Tim's difficult journey to college. At age 9 Tim said to Joanie one night, "Something's wrong with me." Joanie says, "He got out of bed and took me around the house and showed me all the things he had to do before he could sleep." His obsessive-compulsive disorder, attention issues, and other learning difficulties made elementary school a hellish experience, as did the long and painful search to find the right physician and combination of learning supports, therapy, and medication. Tim's dad also helped, but it has been Joanie's inexhaustible determination and love, along with Tim's own resilience and ambition, that have carried him to college. Now in his first year he receives math and reading remediation through the college's tutoring program. Yet Joanie finds it hard to stop calling and texting her son several times a day. Worry, habit, and her cell phone drive Joanie, even though she knows better. "I've realized that I don't want Tim to feel he can't do things on this own." But, she says, looking at Tim for his reaction, "It's a hard thing to deal with. I struggle all the time. I have a long way to go." In response Tim grins and says, "I want less calls."

As Joanie so movingly shows, years of advocating and anxiety, amplified by a cell phone, can make it tougher for these parents and students to figure out how to maintain a healthy connection with each other. For these families it's vital to anticipate how college will differ from high school and how parents can help their children learn to become their own best advocates as they work toward adulthood.

## From High School to College: An Abrupt Transition

Many families of students with challenges experience a shock when the child moves from high school to college. Until a child reaches college age, federal law (the Individuals with Disabilities Education Act) requires school districts to educate each child with a disability and provide services that ensure an equitable education. A school district must identify and meet the educational needs of a child with a disability as well as it meets the needs of students without disabilities. Notably the law also guarantees that parents can have a voice in the process.

All that changes after high school. A different law covers students who continue schooling after they turn 18: the Americans with Disabilities Act (ADA), which views them as adults. Before college, school officials and parents advocate for students' needs. In college, students must become their own advocates. If students choose to ask for services or accommodations, they must provide necessary documentation. Accommodations for academic coursework are handled on a case-by-case basis, depending not only on the individual's needs but on the particular requirements of each course. (If a course has only untimed or take-home exams, for example, the professor doesn't need to know that a student qualifies for extra time on tests.)

These differences between high school and college are enormous. Dr. Jane E. Jarrow, a consultant to colleges on disability issues (whose daughter is a college student with cerebral palsy and limited speech), puts it this way: "The responsibility of the K-12 system is to provide success to kids with disabilities." But after high school the emphasis shifts to *access*, she said. Under ADA qualified students with documented disabilities are entitled to equal access to the same educational opportunities that students without disabilities have. Educators must provide "reasonable accommodations" to qualified students. Typically these include additional time on tests, distraction-free environments for test taking, and note-taking and reading services, depending on the student's condition and the course. The law encompasses services to those with a full spectrum of disabilities and also includes building code requirements regarding physical access and mobility.

Another seismic shift in college is that parents are no longer a part of the ongoing conversation. There are no more IEPs, the Individual Educational Plan mandated by law in a child's earlier years. "Right up until kids graduate from high school, parents are required by law to be consulted," said Jarrow, a spirited advocate for the disabled. In those years parents can meet regularly with guidance counselors, school psychologists, teachers, and administrators. Calls and emails may fly back and forth. With the increase in computer-based reporting programs, many parents receive frequent updates on their kids' homework, class participation, and quiz scores, which can help parents monitor the success of an IEP. ("Uh-oh, Diane got a C- on her Algebra II quiz today. Maybe we need to meet with the teacher to see if the accommodations are working.")

This changes overnight. "At the college level, parents have no rights," said Jarrow. "Not only is their opinion not necessary, it may not be welcome, for the most part. It's very different from the K-12 system in which 'We will not do anything unless we get parents' approval.' Now we're telling them all of a sudden, 'Your opinion doesn't matter.'" Now what matters is the *student's* perspective, so students have to learn how to advocate for themselves.

## How Parents Respond

Understandably many parents are upset at being sidelined, and some try to take matters into their own hands. Even before classes start, a steady drumbeat of calls, texts, and emails echoes between students and parents about course selections, professors, and accommodations. After the semester begins the tempo increases as parents worry about papers, quizzes, and exams and whether students are getting to morning classes without parents dynamiting them out of bed. Some parents rush too quickly to intervene: "You got a C- on the calculus exam?! You need to see your professor tomorrow! Did you get the extra time that you were supposed to?" Some parental checking-in is appropriate, but nagging never seems to work in the long term, and kids despise it. Knowing when to prompt and how to help the student address the problem can be far more effective. Try something like, "You must have been disappointed to have gotten a C-," and wait for the response. Allow your child to explain what might have gone wrong and to generate solutions, with you as a supportive listener.

*Hiring Tutors*

Some anxious parents take more aggressive action to make sure their child measures up. A few hire independent tutors outside the college to work directly with their child. Sometimes this can fail spectacularly, especially if the student isn't on board with the plan. A dean of first-year students at a very competitive liberal arts college tells of a family who hired a tutor to work with their son, who had documented learning disabilities. The son wasn't giving the tutor the information from his courses. His family was checking in with the tutor and then began to call a student who shared classes with their son, requesting that she provide class notes, a copy of the syllabus, and upcoming assignments to the tutor. According to the dean, the other student said, "The parents call me all the time, . . . They bring me gifts and tell me not to tell anybody they had hired one of these private tutors." The dean and others also suspected the tutor was writing the young man's papers, but couldn't prove it. She confronted the family about the situation and, ultimately, the student, who was very embarrassed by his parents' behavior, withdrew from the college.

Helping to provide tutoring is not a bad idea in some cases, especially when the student is agreeable to it. But students can generally make these arrangements on their own, which then helps them create a relationship with the tutor and take responsibility for the outcome.

### Parents Serving as Tutors

In some cases parents take on the tutoring themselves, just as they did in high school. They overstep their bounds by rewriting papers, prepping their kids for tests over the phone, and helping with research, basically continuing the kind of support they gave in the earlier years. In the parents' eyes, their assistance is helping their kid get good grades. However, the student isn't the one who has earned those grades—and she often knows that—nor has she learned the material. The long-term effects of continuing this practice into college are even more damaging.

One of the best ways parents can help is to find the resources to address their child's specific challenges in the years before college, and gradually taper off the help at home before their child goes to college. Once their child is in college, parents need to learn about the services on campus to assist students and encourage their child to seek help if he or she needs it. Rarely are individuals likely to get as much dedicated assistance for improving their writing and learning skills as they are in college. So it makes sense to let that happen, even if their grades aren't perfect. Parents who try to protect their kids from such learning may be holding them back.

*Parents Calling and Calling*

Another parental strategy is simply to call the college to intervene, whether or not such calls are welcomed by school officials. Disability officers, academic advising deans, and other support staff are deluged with calls and emails from worried parents well before school starts. Rather than responding to parents' concerns, college faculty and administrators would much rather hear directly from the students themselves about academic matters. When it comes to talking to parents about grades and performance issues, college administrators are also worried about violating FERPA, the Family Educational Rights and Privacy Act, a law that gives parents rights with respect to their children's education records in the earlier years, and then transfers those rights to the students at age 18 or when they enter a postsecondary institution.

Under FERPA parents may have access to their kids' academic records with their children's consent. Also, under FERPA colleges may, but aren't required to, grant parents access if their children are parents' confirmed tax dependents. "While college faculty and administrators often would rather work directly with students about academic issues, they recognize parents' level of involvement in their students' lives and are becoming more amenable to parents' requests to access their children's academic records to the extent that FERPA permits," said Nancy Tribbensee, General Counsel for the Arizona University System and FERPA expert. Colleges and universities vary in their policies and typically the registrar's office or dean of students will be able to able to answer families' questions. We recommend that parents and students address this issue before college begins.

Disability officers may be sympathetic to parents' anxieties, but the reality is that parents who call too often and too aggressively may not get the response they want. Certainly most college officials will respond to a true emergency, but frequent and intense calls tend to muddy the waters about what's really a crisis. Larry Powell, the equal opportunity services manager in disability resources at Carnegie Mellon University, often tells parents, "If you advocate too hard for your child, people's eyes are going to glaze over at some point." Some parents find it hard to hit the right note. Their continued involvement helped get their child into college, and they may see no reason to back off now. Colleges, on the other hand, want parents to step back so that students can learn to assert themselves. Parents may share this goal, but may be operating on a different timeline, or they may worry that, if they do back off, their child won't know how to make the transition successfully.

The main lesson here is a basic one: there's a radical divide between high school and college, and families need to recognize it and plan ahead. Stephan Hamlin-Smith, executive director of the Association on Higher Education and Disability, says, "One of the greatest services that a parent can provide to assist their child for college is to prepare them for how very different the rules and operations of colleges are."

## Anticipating How to Respond to Problems

Colleges vary considerably in the support they offer, so it pays to investigate what services are available during the application process. Some things can be counted on, and other services may vary. "Sure (colleges) are willing to give them extra time to take a test, but there isn't the complement of supports and services. We hear more that there aren't sufficient services. Students have to ask and push for those," says George Jesien, executive director of the Association of University Centers on Disabilities.

Once kids have chosen a college and before the first semester starts, they need to identify and find out how to get access to appropriate resources on or near campus. For students with learning disabilities, typical resources include on-site tutors in various subjects, writing centers, note-taking services, and first-year student study skills courses, all of which can be found through the college's disability office. Students also have to learn how to alert a disability officer if they are not getting the accommodations to which they are entitled. Faculty members often have limited information and, unlike many K-12 teachers, generally receive no training about disabilities and accommodations, so they take their cues from disability officers.

For students with medical and psychiatric issues, they and their family may want to connect with the school's counseling and health services, depending on the severity of the problem. Students with medical conditions such as diabetes or epilepsy may also want to consider alerting the college's resident life office. Student support groups at school are another option to consider.

Parents can work out in advance how they can help support their children while at the same time also encouraging their children to be responsible for their health and behavior. For some that support might mean that parents agree to handle insurance paperwork to pay for insulin supplies or medications. The student can be responsible for making and attending physician or counseling appointments, as well as maintaining a healthy lifestyle of good diet and exercise. Clarifying these roles before college helps to alleviate some of the tension of phone calls during college.

Although many students continue working with their health care providers at home, they need a backup plan on campus for prescriptions, medical supplies, therapists, and physicians. For example, students with diabetes need on-site sources for replacing lost blood monitors, malfunctioning pumps, or dwindling insulin supplies. That means locating pharmacies near campus before the semester starts. Face-to-face contact with a counselor or learning specialist at school may also prove helpful, so students need to learn what counseling and learning centers can offer. If the centers do not provide the level of help that the student needs they can often suggest referrals in the community. Students recovering from cancer or other serious illnesses may want to establish a backup relationship with a physician near campus.

Parents may also want to know whom to contact in the event that they sense a real problem with their child. That means figuring out the go-to person in the dorm's resident advisor system and getting the phone number and email address. Given the increasing absence of landlines in dorms, it's also helpful to get the cell phone number of a roommate or best friend, though parents need to assure their kids that they will call those students only in the event of a true emergency. If something does go wrong, parents will be very glad to have those contacts in hand.

## The First-Semester Transition

The first semester is a huge transition. For most students, college is their first independent (relatively speaking) living experience. Sometimes students with parents who have helped them manage a learning disorder, physical disability, or illness get to college and react by nudging the parents away. They might also recognize this as a time to take charge of their own well-being. Meanwhile the involved parents may try to hang on rather than celebrate the move toward autonomy. Parents need to think hard about whose needs are being met in their desire for such frequent contact.

For some students with disabilities this new independence means upholding the privacy of their educational records (even if parents would prefer such access). For others, it's refusing to call their parents as frequently as the parents want.

Jane Daigneault, associate director of academic advising and co-ordinator of disability services at Clark University in Worcester, is well versed in cases where students and parents have opposing views on what the parents' involvement should be. She recalls one student with a learning disability who had taken a year off before starting at Clark, spending his gap year abroad. The summer before he arrived at college, his parents called and emailed Daigneault constantly about services for their son's learning disability. When they all met in her office the following fall, the son told his parents he wouldn't sign a FERPA waiver. During his gap year he had managed life on his own, doing laundry and getting meals, and now, he said, he could do college on his own. (He had done fine abroad, after all.)

The mother was shocked, according to Daigneault. "She said, 'I plan on calling you every day,' and the boy said, 'I won't be answering you every day.' The mother cried. This is her youngest child going off to college and she was very upset by the whole thing. And the dad said, 'What if you would email every day, or what if you text us daily just so we know you're okay?'" The son refused. His progression toward independence was well under way and he wanted no backsliding. Finally Daigneault helped negotiate a compromise: the son would call home twice a week.

The student sought the services he needed, and he did fabulously. "He met with me every week for a full year," Daigneault said. "He didn't want [his parents] overshadowing him every day, and he knew the benefit of coming over to this office." Taking charge of his own situation, against the wishes of his parents, was in his own best interests.

Other cases end not so happily, particularly when parents try to compensate for their child's disability by keeping an eye on him and the student fights back by withdrawing from them. This is what happened to Jason and his parents, according to his mother's account. Jason was diagnosed with attention-deficit hyperactivity disorder (ADHD) at 5 and given medication to increase his focus and organization skills. "With ADHD kids, you really have to stay on top of them," his mom said. "Though in our son's case he would become resentful."

Jason did well enough to get admitted to a more selective liberal arts college. The school had numerous resources for students like Jason, and he and his parents met with the school's disability office to arrange weekly one-on-one sessions to help Jason manage his time and organize his course load. But just before Thanksgiving Jason began skipping his meds and his weekly meetings, challenging whether he really had the disorder, something that he had argued with his parents about before college. He had agreed to call or videochat with his parents twice a week, which he also stopped doing.

Fearful, his parents called the disability officer, who actually drove to Jason's room, at the parents' insistence, and got him to call them on the spot. When he stopped calling again after Thanksgiving, his parents were both anxious and annoyed, and repeatedly called the college's disability office to see if he was attending classes. The office confirmed that he was, but had no other information. To Jason's parents, hundreds of miles away, it was as if he had vanished: no calls, texts, or emails for three weeks. Finally they called campus security, which sent an officer to his room. He found Jason there, perfectly fine, at least on the surface.

The semester didn't end well, with Jason withdrawing from one class and failing another. "When he realized he couldn't function, he couldn't admit it to us. It was a total disaster," said his mother, frustrated at his inability to take advantage of the extensive help available at the college. "I was hoping that he would have a little more maturity." The parents insisted he return home to live and attend a local college, where he has enjoyed some success.

Jason's parents were frustrated with his experience at his first college. His mother commented, "Where they fall short is that whole thing that 'they are adults now.' Come on! He is an eighteen-year-old kid with this disorder. They didn't say, 'Jason, you didn't show up. Why didn't you show up?'" Most colleges reasonably expect that students are ready to make the commitment or experience the consequences and don't need their parents or professors making sure they attend class. Some students might be better off postponing college until they are ready for the responsibilities (without mom serving as the alarm clock anymore), or attend a small college where lack of attendance often gets noticed and is not simply considered a student's prerogative. In any college setting, learning to accept the consequences is also a part of growing up. This kind of experimentation with the limits is not uncommon, especially among kids who find college to be the first place where they are given any choices.

When parents take on too much for their children, kids don't learn to take responsibility. Jason had already questioned his diagnosis, and in college he doubted it further. Jason might have benefited from reviewing his diagnosis with a therapist or doctor, or considered further testing. Lacking the certainty about his condition or the skills to do his work successfully in the new freedom of college, Jason was unable to function as a student. He ended up back at home, with both he and his family feeling badly about his first college experience.

## Getting and Accepting a Diagnosis

Kids need to make peace with their diagnoses, as do parents. In the best of worlds this occurs before college. Sometimes learning disabilities aren't evident until the workload outstrips the student's ability to compensate. When Barbara was teaching a course as a graduate student at the University of Michigan, a first-year student was actually relieved when she saw her very low score on a reading test given in class. It explained, she said, why she had had to spend twice as long as her friends keeping up with the assigned reading in high school. Now in college there simply weren't enough hours to read as much as she needed to. She had begun to fall behind, so it helped to find the reason. She then learned how to compensate through a referral to the learning and reading skills center.

Other students may have had similar conditions diagnosed late in high school. Today more students than ever face some kind of challenge, but they may not share it with their peers or with college officials. Some may want to see what they can handle in this new environment. It's not uncommon for students to take a wait-and-see attitude before they decide whether to submit documentation to a disabilities officer.

Getting an adolescent on the brink of adulthood to accept a diagnosis can be difficult, but it's even more difficult when the parents are ambivalent about it too. Some parents may downplay their child's disability, giving him or her little information about it. Even in families who disclose their child's learning disabilities, some students have no clue about what their disabilities really are or which accommodations to seek. "Some parents want to protect their children and not let them read their reports [about their disabilities]," said Jodi Litchfield, the Americans with Disabilities Act coordinator for Middlebury College. The first time some students learn in detail about their problem is when they read their documentation in the college's disability office.

Parents who fear that students with special needs might be treated prejudicially sometimes decide they don't want their kids to be identified by the college. Some of these children end up realizing it would be better to come forward with their needs and receive the accommodations they are permitted by law.

## How Schools Respond

Schools often find themselves in the middle, between parents and students, trying their best to meet the family's different needs. Many disability officers, tutors, therapists, and physicians purposely keep parents at arm's length. "Our primary relationship is with the student," says Jeff Orgera, whose SALT program at the University of Arizona helps students individually with organization, time management, and study skills. "We can't have a productive relationship if the student feels we are calling the parents." This is especially true for students receiving psychological counseling on campus. Without a student's consent, physicians and therapists will typically not talk to parents unless the student is an imminent risk to herself or others. Naturally if parents have vital information about their children and if their children have given consent, therapists may listen to the parents' concerns, but by and large they won't discuss specifics about their patients.

Orgera and other experts with whom we talked see their role as being quietly supportive rather than actively engaged in the students' ongoing tutoring, therapy, or other treatment. For parents who enjoyed close relationships with their child's high school teachers or local pediatrician, this more distant relationship may take some getting used to. Parenting an emerging adult is definitely different from parenting an adolescent.

## Taking Ownership

Students who take charge of their health or learning challenge tend to do better than their peers who don't, say students and disability officers with whom we talked at various colleges. Heather, a student at Louisiana State University, has struggled with her ADHD since elementary school and is still working through its complexities. With expert help, medication, and pure grit, she has learned to compensate. Her parents' acceptance has been invaluable. In middle school she received intensive help to develop study skills, which has proved a real asset in college. She also knows when she learns best and schedules accordingly: "This semester I scheduled classes from seven-thirty a.m. to twelve-thirty p.m. I know myself. A lot of times I would go to bed at nine p.m. and get up at four a.m. to study. An hour of me studying in the morning is worth two of me at night."

The early-morning schedule has its drawbacks. Heather can't party the night before her 7:30 a.m. class, even though her sorority sisters and friends in the dorm do. But she is comfortable with her decision. "That's one of the things mom helped me with. I have a learning disability and my body can't handle going out." As she learned from playing tennis in high school, Heather uses exercise to increase her ability to focus, kickboxing and running regularly. "If I was studying for two hours and would run, then I could study about one hour more." Because she has trouble with organization, she uses a strategy from middle school, color-coding all her notebooks and assignments: purple for calculus, and so on.

Heather's parents are highly educated professionals and have worked hard to prepare her for an increasingly independent life at LSU, even though they would have preferred a smaller school for her. Her mom helped her through the admissions process, but not by doing the work for her: "If I felt she wasn't doing enough research, I made an appointment with the high school counselor and he just blasted her. I refused to do it for her. I would do it with her, but not for her." Before she left for college, her parents also tried to ready her for the practical side of campus life. For Heather's senior year in high school they gave her a reasonable sum to cover her clothing and book costs. It was up to her to budget it; as part of that process they taught her how to balance a checkbook.

Heather visits home once a month and talks to her family about four times a week, which recently included a webcam visit to see her dog and a text from her dad: "'Hope you have a great day and luv you!' It's really cute that he spells it wrong," she said affectionately.

Heather's mom says her daughter initiates calls more than she does. "She's very independent. I don't know what she's doing every day," she says. She is proud of her daughter's budding autonomy, despite a rocky start. In her first semester Heather suffered from homesickness and nearly failed a demanding course, which she had the misfortune of taking at night. During that time her parents encouraged her to keep advocating for herself, giving suggestions and strategies: "Mostly we've offered a lot of emotional support." Heather has been a strong advocate for herself, seeking as much help as she can get by attending every available weekly study session for her classes. She is still working to adapt her disorder to a college environment. "I don't have it completely figured out," she says. She is also learning more about herself. "I'm still searching for who I am. I realized I had to find out who I am to become more independent and mature and to take things into my own hands. It's very hard to do."

Heather's parents did a great job helping her prepare for college. Their life skills lessons on managing money are invaluable for all students, but especially those with learning issues. Tim, who we met earlier, got a lot of calls from his mom when he overdrew his account. Before college Tim had had little practice with an ATM card or his own checking account.

Heather's parents also helped her to gradually learn to manage her own learning challenge. Larry Powell of Carnegie Mellon University says, "One of the traps that some parents of students with a disability fall into is that they don't give students adequate opportunity for managing their disability before they come to college. What that means is now all of a sudden the child wants to be cut loose and they haven't prepared the child for this or haven't prepared themselves. There needs to be an incremental approach."

Sometimes the idea for an incremental approach comes from the students themselves. Sam, who was diagnosed with ADHD at age 6, did fairly well in school, with medication and support from his family. But in his senior year in high school, he said no more meds. He thought they interfered with his creativity, and he loved acting in his school's improvisational theater. He also wasn't really sure that he had the disorder anymore; he thought he had outgrown it.

His parents were aghast, but after talking with their son's psychologist they decided that it was better to let him try dropping the meds in the last half of his senior year rather than in his first semester of college. "We made a contract with him that if he was going off meds that there were certain things that he would have to demonstrate," his mother said. "We talked about his GPA, cars, and curfews, and not getting any tickets [he had gotten a ticket first semester for speeding]. As part of the contract, we made him read the first five chapters of Dr. Edward Hallowell's book [*Driven to Distraction*]." To their surprise, Sam met their expectations, but they were still anxious about the rigors of college. "I tried to send a bottle of Concerta with him to college," his mom said. But Sam refused to take it.

Sam did well at college, earning a GPA of 4.0. Part of it he credited to studying after his two-hour workouts. The rest came from his determination and following his passions in college: psychology and performing in the school's improv troupe. Even though Sam didn't follow a traditional treatment path, he took charge of his condition, using his assets to compensate and achieve.

For students with complex medical problems such as diabetes, transition efforts should begin well before college. "Diabetes is not a do-it-yourself condition. It always requires support," says Dr. Lori Laffel, chief of the Pediatric, Adolescent and Young Adult Section at the Joslin Diabetes Center. "It's critically important that parents remain engaged; however, the growing adolescent needs to take on more and more responsibility." Laffel's patients and others at Joslin are counseled throughout their senior year in high school about making the move to college. Parents are a key part of the discussion and need to figure out in advance how to best support their children once they are in college. "We encourage them to ask their children, 'How would you like me to help?' and not say what they want to do. We encourage parents to say less and listen more. This *is* an example of when less is more." Because the student's needs may change, this kind of dialogue needs to be ongoing.

Susan, a University of Alabama student with diabetes, advises other students with the disease to start taking charge in high school: "It's a good idea to know how to fill your prescriptions, make your doctor's appointments, go to your doctor's appointment by yourself, to be able to grocery shop for yourself. These things seem really basic but you don't tend to these things until you go to college. I'm not going to lie . . . I love it when my mom does things for me, but I know how to do these things." The same goes for students with psychiatric disabilities and other medical conditions: they can benefit from making their own appointments and filling their own prescriptions.

## Develop a Calling Plan

It's especially important for families to have a plan of when and how they will communicate during the school year. A thoughtful, caring family discussion before a student leaves for college will go a long way toward developing a workable plan. Parents can listen to their child's concerns and express their own. The child may have a better understanding of her parents' perspective if they let her know that college is also a big transition for them. Acknowledging and honoring others' feelings is part of the process of developing into an adult.

Parents who call too frequently can communicate anxiety about their child's ability to successfully manage her new life at college. Parents' anxiety may be understandable, but they need to figure out how to manage it on their own, and if it is debilitating, therapy may be the solution. Parents of students with difficult medical conditions may want to be in more regular contact, but without overdoing it. For example, the physiological and emotional changes of adolescence and emerging adulthood can make managing a college student's diabetes more difficult than when he or she was younger. Those changes, coupled with the competing demands of academics, athletics, and a social life, can make the college years more volatile. Every patient is different, and the disease has varying degrees of severity. As is the case with most such conditions, the level of severity and the patient's overall health should drive parents' level of contact and support, according to Laffel. "You have to find the healthy mix that will make both parties happy."

Clearly some students with more stable conditions may require fewer check-ins and are bolstered by parental trust. It is easy to understand a parent's anxiety, yet children need to know that their parents are confident in their abilities to manage their lives and that they will seek help when they need it. This is their chance to make the transition to adulthood and to manage their own disability, disorder, or medical condition with all the support a college community offers. Take guidance from your child about how much is enough, and don't hesitate to ask if you're unclear what he or she wants. Consider who needs reassurance, you or your growing adult child, and respect his or her needs first.

## Accepting the Bumpy Road

Understandably, many parents will try to help their kids with disabilities avoid predictable bumps in the road, sometimes even small ones best navigated by the student alone. Attempts to manage each small step, perhaps by calling or firing off an email to a professor or a dean, is not the path to take, unless of course a student's health is at stake.

"You have to sometimes allow students to fail," observes Orgera.

"You can't prevent struggle and you can't save or rescue them. There are going to be good days and bad days. If they pick up the phone and call you after every situation they encounter, how are they going to develop problem-solving skills? Each email, phone call, or visit is impeding the student's development because they realize that mom and dad are still coming to the rescue and will fix problems for [them] and make phone calls for [them]. Sometimes parents of students with challenges don't think they can count on students to do those things. But they can." If your children don't know how to take care of these things yet, give them space to learn.

## Advice to Parents

Making the transition from high school to college is a profound adjustment for students with disabilities. In the best of worlds, families may plan for this change well before college. For students with learning disabilities, that means beginning as early as middle school, having students attend school meetings about how to address the educational impacts of their disability, and by the ninth or tenth grade actually having the student help direct those meetings, says Hamlin-Smith, executive director of AHEAD. For students with psychiatric illnesses and medical diseases such as diabetes, it means a gradual shifting of responsibility for the condition, so that the move to college is more of an "evolution" than a revolution, says Laffel, the diabetes expert. Odds are those families will make a smoother transition to college.

Having a child with disabilities in college requires parents to rethink their roles. Parents are no longer their children's formal advocates. It's up to their children now, and whatever parents can do to encourage their children to get the help they need themselves will go a long way. If they haven't already, students need to learn everything they can about their disability. They need to learn what circumstances can aggravate their condition, which accommodations work best for them, and what resources are available to them on or near campus. Even if parents have to role-play with them, students need to learn how to talk articulately about these issues with college faculty, disability administrators, counselors, even roommates.

Parents also need to work out with their kids in advance a regular schedule of communication in line with their children's disability and overall needs. Just as important, parents need to figure out what to say and how to listen to their children in ways that support their development.

## Chapter 9

# Mental Health Issues at College - - - - - - - - - - -

## A Challenge for All Parents

Today the odds are that a college student will either have a roommate, a teammate, or a classmate who has some kind of mental health issue or will experience an issue of his own. Some mental health problems are moderate and temporary, such as a bout of anxiety at midterms, while others are not. Early identification and treatment of more serious conditions, including mood, anxiety, and eating disorders, have enabled students with these problems to attend college. For many of these adolescents, even in the recent past, college would likely have been far less manageable. The fact that these students have made it to college is cause for celebration, but that celebration is tempered with concern on the part of parents, other students, college administrators, and health care professionals. Students with more severe challenges, and their peers who care about them, need to have appropriate resources and support to do well on campus. So do their classmates, who may suffer from milder problems. Parents play a huge role in providing emotional support to their kids and helping them learn about the resources in their college community. But parents struggle to figure out how much support to continue to provide and when to do so. These questions become even tougher to answer when parents and kids are on speed-dial.

For parents of students with mental health issues, it is often more challenging to balance their desire for a close connection with a desire for their child to grow into a competent adult. When their kids head off to college, these parents worry about how they will manage the typical but often stressful adjustments to college life as well as their depression, eating disorder, or anxiety. Their children may share that worry, as may their friends and roommates. Parents also need to know how to support their own kids when they are worried about someone who won't eat or who is unable to get out of bed for three days.

Whether or not a family has a child with a psychological disorder, families of all college students will benefit from learning about basic mental health issues. It's especially important for kids who have a diagnosed problem to be knowledgeable about their own disorder and the resources on campus to address it. College is a time for students to stretch themselves academically, emotionally, and socially, and it's also a time to learn how to keep themselves mentally healthy then and in the years beyond.

## Psychological Disorders on Campus

Psychological disorders are a fact of life on campuses across the country. Some chronic psychiatric conditions, such as anxiety and impulse control disorders, generally surface by the mid-20s. Students may also have eating disorders, depression, and other mood and personality disorders. Alcohol use disorders also are common among college students. Campus counseling centers are continuing to see a rise in students arriving with severe psychological problems, according to a 2009 survey of center directors. The 2007–2009 Healthy Minds Study, an annual national survey of college students, found that 22 percent of students had screened positively for either depression or anxiety in the past year; 15 percent reported purposely hurting themselves, the most common forms of injury being punching themselves, pulling their hair, and hitting objects; 6 percent had considered suicide in the past year, and 1.6 percent admitted to making a plan to do it. Each year, experts estimate, about 1,100 college students actually take their lives.

Other studies reveal reason for concern. For example, nearly one out of three undergrads reported being so depressed at least once in the previous year that they found it difficult to function, according to the Fall 2008 National College Health Assessment sponsored by the American College Health Association. Nearly half of the students reported that they had experienced overwhelming anxiety in the same period. Results from the National Epidemiologic Study on Alcohol and Related Conditions indicate that one in five college students in their study had a problem with alcohol. The Healthy Minds Study also found a high prevalence of concerns with body image and other risk factors for eating disorders. For example, more than one out of three women (37 percent) and about one in six men (16 percent) answered yes to the question "Do you still feel too fat even though others say you are thin?"

"Mental health problems are clearly one of the biggest issues facing young people in the United States," said Dr. Daniel Eisenberg, an assistant professor of health management and policy at the University of Michigan and director of the Healthy Minds Study, a joint effort between the university's school of public health, its comprehensive Depression Center, and the Center for Student Studies. Eisenberg also points to the findings of the World Health Organization's global disease study, which shows that "mental and behavioral disorders account for the largest burden of disorders for young people in the United States." What concerns Eisenberg and other mental health professionals is that many students aren't receiving treatment. For example, the Healthy Minds Study found that fewer than half of the students who screened positively for mood or anxiety disorders had received any treatment in the previous year.

When students are depressed or anxious at school they are more likely to tell a friend than anyone else, including family members, according to a 2004 survey of about a thousand college students and about a thousand parents of college students by the National Alliance on Mental Illness and Abbott Laboratories. Schools are raising awareness about mental illness among students, faculty, and parents and working to erase the shame associated with it. Since 2005 more than ninety colleges have received $22 million in federal funds for suicide prevention and mental health awareness programs, according to the U.S. Substance Abuse and Mental Health Services Administration.

At Tufts University activities at its popular parents' weekend in October now include a talk about students' mental health issues. At the University of Minnesota college administrators, from the top down, have been waging a multiyear campaign called "Stamp Out Stigma," with speeches from the president, posters in student bathrooms, and a student art show. Active Minds, Inc., a nonprofit organization dedicated to mental health awareness and wiping out the disgrace surrounding mental health issues, now has at least 240 student-run chapters at colleges across the country. (Its website is www.activeminds.org.) On campus a new attitude toward mental illness is emerging. "It's a lot more tolerant and accepting of mental health issues than in my day," said Dr. Ronald C. Albucher, a psychiatrist and director of Counseling and Psychological Services at Stanford University. "Students themselves are much more open about it. It's much healthier." Some students write about personal psychological struggles on their college applications.

Overall this new campus landscape may alarm some parents, whose instinct may be to check in constantly with their children. Experts on the campus front lines of mental health recommend certain behaviors that all parents practice. Calling constantly is not one of them.

## Recommendations for Parents

*Talk about Mental Illness Issues before Children Go to College*
According to the National Alliance on Mental Illness, many students arrive at college knowing little about mental health issues. Mental health experts recommend that before their child leaves for campus parents talk honestly with him about depression and anxiety in a calm and nonjudgmental way, just as they might discuss the issues of alcohol and substance abuse. This is especially important for students whose family members may have a history of alcoholism or other psychiatric illness that may put these students at greater risk for developing these disorders. The idea is to begin a dialogue so that the child will be comfortable talking to his mom and dad if later he feels overwhelmingly sad or anxious or becomes very concerned about a friend. A good way to start is to ask kids how they feel about heading off to college and to let them know that it's normal to feel a little anxious or worried. Sharing your own experiences of excitement and anxiety about a new job or your own early days in college can also open up the conversation. Let your kids know that you are always available if they feel depressed or worried or have trouble eating or sleeping. Also tell them that help is available in a safe and private environment at the college counseling center, and explain how that is paid for.

While most parents know in their gut when something is amiss with their child, it's worth learning about some red flags. The Tufts University website for their Counseling and Mental Health Center provides faculty and staff with a list of warning signs for recognizing when a student is in distress. Some of these signs, which would alert a faculty or staff member to refer the student to the counseling center, are ones parents might also be alert to:

- Depressed or lethargic mood
- Hyperactivity
- Increased or excessive alcohol or drug use
- Sleeping problems (either too much or too little)
- Feeling worthless
- Expressions of hopelessness
- Rambling or incoherent speech
- Social withdrawal
- Apathy
- Inability to concentrate
- Excessive anxiety

Parents can also let their kids know where to turn if they or their friends have a problem. The most convenient and practical sources of support are right on campus: a residence advisor, the college's counseling or student health center, or the Dean of Students Office. At the University of Texas at Austin students and faculty members can call in to a Behavior Concerns Advice Line or register their concerns online. In case of a real emergency, such as a threatened suicide or a stalker, students should call the campus or community police.

### Advice for Parents of Students with a History of Psychological Disorders

For families whose child already has a diagnosed disorder, experts offer more specific recommendations. First, parents and their child's therapist and physician can assess whether the child is well enough to tackle college and all the stresses associated with the first-year transition. "Sometimes a parent will call up and say 'My daughter or son just got out of the hospital for an eating disorder or depression or some other psychiatric illness, or recently tried to kill himself or herself. And I want you to note that this is going on,'" said Dr. Mark McLeod, director of the student counseling center at Emory University in Georgia. "I'll say, 'Have you thought of waiting to really make sure your kid is okay?' and the parent will say, 'I can't believe that you guys are telling me my child shouldn't come here.' The bottom line is that this is not a safe place for students in this phase of their illness." Some parents heed his advice. Parents need to work closely with the mental health provider to make a decision in the best interest of the child. Some colleges are willing to defer admission under such circumstances.

If students are healthy enough for college, they and their parents need to have some straightforward discussions. Honesty is the place to start. Marilyn Downs, outreach director at the Counseling and Mental Health Service at Tufts University, suggests this kind of frankness from a parent: "This is my first time doing this too, and I don't really know how I'll feel when you walk out that door. But I just want the best for you, and we'll have to figure this out as we go along. I'll make some mistakes, and you're going to have let me know whether I'm too involved or not involved enough."

The dialogue also needs to address clinical aspects of the child's disorder. For example, Dr. Chris Brownson, director of the Counseling and Mental Health Center of the University of Texas at Austin, says, "If a student has a history of depression, parents need to have a conversation with their child before college about recognizing the warning signs of depression based on their previous experience." While there are common symptoms for depression, individuals are unique, and the disorder may manifest itself a little differently in each person. "First, the students need to recognize what their symptoms are and secondly, what to do when they notice them. The earlier you can recognize that these symptoms are emerging, the quicker you can get help and increase the odds of a better outcome."

Before school begins parents also need to get in touch with therapists and physicians at the college's counseling center and, with their child's permission, let them know about their child's condition. Increasingly, more families are making this kind of contact. At Stanford, Albucher is seeing more parents and students visiting his center during orientation week. At Emory, McLeod says, "Oftentimes we will get parents who call us and will say 'My son or daughter has this history of anxiety or depression.' We like that. That makes it easier for the kids to get in touch with us through their parents or on their own." Depending on the individual student, the counseling center staff can help the family make other helpful connections.

"If there's a strong concern, we may suggest the parents and student let the residence life people know. If there are some learning disabilities [along with the disorder], we may suggest some conversations about academic supports with our learning center," McLeod adds. The student's buy-in is essential, and parents should involve their children in this process. "You want a student and particularly an eighteen-year-old student to have a feeling of control, and allowing them to participate fully in the discussions with the school will help achieve that."

Students and their parents also need to be at peace with their diagnosis and care. If students have doubts, they need to be listened to respectfully, by a professional. One of the most effective ways to help people accept the diagnosis of a psychological disorder is to emphasize that it is a legitimate medical illness, said Dr. Gary Christenson, a psychiatrist and director of the Mental Health Clinic at the University of Minnesota's Boynton Health Service.

## Arranging for Help

College counseling centers are generally set up to provide emergency and short-term therapy. Typically they provide anywhere from four to fifteen sessions in a year, but students in nonemergency situations may have to wait several days for appointments at most schools, according to Dr. Robert Gallagher, author of the annual National Survey of Counseling Directors. For students needing longer term treatment, the centers are good referral sources for therapists in the surrounding community. Parents may also want to ask their child's treating physician at home to work with the new therapist. "Most adolescents don't want to change physicians right before the transition to college. It doesn't feel like the right time to do it," said Dr. Lisa Namerow, a child and adolescent psychiatrist, specializing in medical and developmental disabilities at the Institute of Living at Hartford Hospital in Connecticut. Namerow tells her patients, "'I want to know how you are doing and I need to touch base with your therapist.' Actually as a treating psychiatrist, I can connect to a therapist in more legal ways than parents can." Once students are 18 they are considered adults and their medical records are private. Unless they have students' consent, a college's physicians and therapists in general may not talk to parents about their children's medical issues. Of course, if these medical professionals consider these students an imminent threat to themselves or others, they may talk about their treatment of these students to their parents. And if parents have vital information about their children, therapists want to receive it—with their patients' permission. Therapists won't discuss what goes on in therapy, which requires trust and rapport between a patient and a therapist, and that can't happen if a parent is allowed to hear what's said in a private therapy session.

### The Promise and Problem of a Fresh Start

Some families see college as a fresh start and a chance to put their child's mental health issues in the past. Gary Christenson at the University of Minnesota knows this scenario all too well: "We find first-year students believing, 'This new life in college means I've already kicked my anxiety or eating disorder.' But they don't prepare themselves for that disorder returning or that it never really went away." College offers many exciting new experiences for students; it also can bring crushing stress. Adjusting to the freedom of a college environment, new roommates, a new sleep schedule, a school meal plan, and more demanding classes is difficult and can worsen existing conditions or trigger a relapse.

Anne, a student at a large midwestern university, suffered from significant depression in high school, but after much therapy and a good senior year thought she could manage college. Her parents did too, not realizing the gravity of Anne's illness. In high school she had contemplated suicide many times, though never explicitly telling them. Once she did try to tell her mom, saying, "I'm just so sad. I can't be here anymore." But her mother looked so upset that Anne felt compelled to keep quiet. "I couldn't let anyone in my family know these things. I thought it would hurt them too much." When it was time for college, Anne's thoughts of suicide had faded and she was excited about the new life ahead. "It was a fresh start. My image of college was one of complete happiness. I would find a million friends and party all the time—and you're free! I thought it was my break, a chance to start over." When Anne's parents finished settling her in her new dorm room, Anne made a show of pushing them out the door. "I wanted to prove myself. This is my first time on my own and I wanted to prove that I could make a life for myself and let my interests flourish."

But Anne's first semester experience proved "completely the opposite": "I felt like a tiny fish in a big sea. I didn't feel connected to anyone in the university." She made a few friends but found her new life discouraging and began to sink into a depression, losing her appetite and passion for school, just as she had done before. "I didn't notice at first that I was becoming depressed," she said. Christmas break was a turning point. "I came home and all my relatives were like, 'You are so thin, so skinny. Don't you just love school?' I didn't have the heart to tell anyone this experience is terrible." She couldn't tell her friends, who all seemed to love college, nor her family, especially because her older sister had loved her college experience. After Christmas Anne went back to school, but she came home every weekend feeling too sad and isolated to stay there. Luckily home was just twenty minutes away. "My mom was sad for me. She knew how I struggled. Every weekend we would take walks together and on those walks she would be quiet. I knew that she was inviting me to speak. Just the fact that she was listening was a help." Her father, she says, has never acknowledged her disorder: "He's uncomfortable with it. It's stigmatized in our society and it's an unknown to him." With the support of a few friends who were open to discussing their own mental health problems, Anne limped through the spring semester. She didn't seek counseling on campus because she wasn't sure whether her insurance would cover it. "It was too scary and overwhelming for me to look into," she said. That summer she went into intensive treatment at home with a new therapist. Eventually she recovered enough to return to college, where with the support of her therapist she became deeply involved in campus life, including the university's Active Minds chapter. Now, even though everything isn't perfect, she is doing much better.

Fortunately Anne finally got the support that she needed. But her experience demonstrates the need for parents and students with psychological disorders to stay aware of their illness's symptoms and to learn how to access the resources available on campus. Anne could have sought help on campus, but didn't know how to. To be fair, her parents didn't realize the depth of her illness, or that it had returned. Though Anne didn't say how ill she was, her behavior showed it. College is a chance for a new beginning, but families need to prepare for the possibility that an illness may resurface, especially with the stress of moving from high school to college.

*Parents Need to Keep Perspective*

Sometimes parents are well aware of their child's disorder but let their own hopes and fears cloud their judgment. Sometimes parents don't understand the complexities of their child's disorder.

Jocelyn, for example, developed anorexia in her high school years. Everyone at her small, private high school—students, faculty, and administrators—knew about her disorder and formed a protective cocoon around her. ("The school nurse let me keep yogurt in her fridge," Jocelyn recalled.) An only child, Jocelyn was very close to her parents, who made sure she received therapy. When she applied to one of the nation's most selective universities, she didn't tell college officials about her disorder. "My mom told me not to say anything because she was afraid they wouldn't take me," she said.

When she was admitted she maintained the silence, at the urging of her parents and therapist: "They felt very strongly that I should go away and build an identity separate from my eating disorder." But when she got to college that was a harder task than she or her parents had imagined. "I didn't know quite what to say to people or who to tell. I felt like I was hiding from something all the time. Basically my therapist told me not to say anything unless absolutely necessary. I ended up feeling kind of isolated."

Instead of finding a new therapist at college, Jocelyn decided to continue counseling through phone sessions with her therapist at home. Closeted from her peers and without face-to-face support, she became clinically depressed and relapsed. "I wouldn't eat the food. It would taste like cardboard. I lost a significant amount of weight." Eventually she wound up leaving college and taking a year off while she received intensive therapy with a new therapist. Young women with eating disorders can reinforce each other's destructive dieting. Perhaps Jocelyn's therapist and family counseled her to be quiet about her disorder hoping that she wouldn't find this kind of destructive influence in her new college environment. But the advice also grew from their fear that disclosing her eating disorder would hurt her chances for admission to a prestigious college. Complex and poignant, Jocelyn's experience shows the difficulties of managing a disorder in a culture that stigmatizes mental illness. It also shows that once on campus Jocelyn needed support for an ongoing condition.

Eating disorders expert Dr. Margo Maine has counseled many patients and their families about the challenges of college. Even though Jocelyn wasn't her patient, her predicament resonated with Maine: "If you go to college with an active eating disorder, you go with a lot of shame and embarrassment. You are wrapped in a kind of fog that few people will be able to penetrate." Jocelyn's decision to keep her disorder to herself made her college adjustment even more stressful. "If you have a problem that's a secret to everybody, it takes a lot of emotional and physical energy to manage it. It's really going to interfere with all the positive aspects of college life. College is a time to discover yourself and to taste new things—places, people, ideas, relationships, approaches to life. But an eating disorder keeps the person from being able to partake in this new world, literally blunting their ability to taste all these new experiences. . . . Once you have an eating disorder, you realize how little people understand about them and how much shame and stigma remains about these and other mental health problems."

The decision to disclose a psychiatric diagnosis is an intensely personal one. For students with eating disorders that decision often depends on the severity of the illness. Maine says, "If a student is still actively being treated for an eating disorder, parents, to be safe, should disclose the eating disorder to the college's health services, counseling center, or disability office. If the student is at a point where the eating disorder is not a primary problem, where it's not interfering with physical health, parents can consider not disclosing it." Jocelyn, who later enrolled in another prestigious college, did tell this college's disability office about her struggle with depression and her eating disorder. For her it was the right decision. And she made the contact herself. The school's disability office was able to secure accommodations for her while she adjusted to her new antidepression medications, but without telling her professors what the specific problem was, thus safeguarding her privacy.

## Erasing the Stigma of Mental Illness

At the University of Minnesota college officials have been working hard to erase that stigma from the campus culture. Barbara Blacklock, the university's program coordinator for disability services, has been at the front lines of the campaign. "Last year we worked with sixteen hundred students in the disability office and of that group, six hundred had psychiatric disabilities, mostly Generalized Anxiety Disorder and Major Depressive Disorder," she said. Blacklock believes that more students are seeking help thanks to the school's campaign "Stamp Out Stigma." The misinformation and stereotypes associated with psychological issues often place a heavier burden on these students than on those with medical concerns such as diabetes. "One student told me, 'I put my [psychiatric] meds in the bathroom and the roommate came out and said, "I didn't know you were that crazy!"' . . . Parents worry about their students not being able to make friends or having trouble sleeping [due to their medications or the result of noisy dorm life]. This whole umbrella of stigma complicates it. Is their illness going to impact their employability in the future? If someone finds out, how will that affect them?"

### The Parents' Role

Making sure their kids are aware of their disorder and receive the expert care they need is part of the parents' role. Parents also may feel responsible for personally providing what they think is appropriate care and staying in close contact with their child away from home, but our experts say this generally isn't helpful. Studies show that students are more likely to talk about a mental health issue with a peer rather than a parent, and that raises the important question of why.

The reasons are many. "The student may be embarrassed, or worried that their parents might disapprove of their behavior, especially if drugs and alcohol are involved," said Brownson. "The student may feel shame associated with what they are experiencing. Also, culturally there may be some topics that they don't feel are appropriate to discuss with parents. And in the past, they may have not received from parents the kind of support that they needed." Parents may be in denial or ambivalent about their child's problem.

The key is to create and sustain the kind of dialogue that children welcome and that makes them as comfortable sharing their feelings with parents as with friends. Parents need to know that despite their best intentions to have open communication with their kids, this may not happen. "The parent needs to make sure the student is aware of other sources of support on campus and the surrounding community. Because your paramount concern as a parent is that the child is getting the help that they need—not that you are giving it," Brownson said. Help might include counseling, medication, and working with the disabilities office, and perhaps reducing their course load.

## How Much Contact Is Enough? Quantity versus Quality

During the first semester parents may want to be in more frequent contact with their children than later on in college. Because every case is different, the amount of contact can be determined by the child and parent in consultation with the child's therapist or treating physician, rather than parents making this decision alone.

For example, suddenly changing how much parents and children communicate sends the wrong message to the child. Experts with whom we talked all agreed that parents need to think carefully about what and how they communicate with their kids. Parents who call too frequently can communicate anxiety about their child's ability to successfully manage her new life at college. "How parents manage their anxiety is a key factor in how their child does in recovery," said Maine. Instead of helping, too many worried calls undermine a child's confidence. Rather than calling so often, Maine suggests that parents consider seeking the help of a therapist to manage their own anxiety.

But again, frequency isn't the answer. "It's the quality of the contact," says Brownson. "You can talk every day and a student can be experiencing problems and not communicate them to parents. . . . We have some students who may be in very frequent contact with parents, but choose never to discuss their mental health issue, and consequently the parent has no idea what's going on."

To develop that kind of quality communication, Marilyn Downs, the outreach director at Tufts, suggests that parents start by demonstrating a genuine interest in their child's life. Phone calls can sound more like this: "Tell me how your day was. How was your class? And your boyfriend?" And not like this: "How are your grades? Why are you doing *that*? Did you do that?" Downs said, "For most young people I would be hard pressed to think of someone who wouldn't want to have a parent interested in their lives. Most kids want to talk to parents when it feels like this," she said. "In relationships where parents are pressuring them and worrying about academic outcomes, if things go badly, these kids aren't telling their parents."

Parents also can demonstrate their support. Gary Christenson gives a few examples: "Call me anytime if I can be of any help. If I can be of assistance trying to figure out how to navigate the college system, call me."

*Develop a Calling Plan*
It's especially important for families to agree on a plan of when and how they will communicate during the school year. Having a regu-

lar schedule will give parents a baseline of information on how their children are faring. If a student calls or texts regularly and then stops, parents will know that something may be amiss and have a legitimate reason to check in. On the other hand, if a student is calling three or four times a day, that frequency may be a communication about dependence, indecisiveness, homesickness, depression, or anxiety, said Christenson.

Sometimes, though, when students are having acute problems, parents may need to stay more involved, for the student's benefit. That need for monitoring is understandable, and as long as it's reasonable and limited to occasions that warrant it, students are likely to accept the concern and appreciate it.

*Listening Carefully*

Parents do need to listen carefully to what their children are saying and how they are saying it. "If you're noticing a change in behavior in a student, if they don't sound the way they normally do, you need to be direct," says Mark McLeod at Emory. "I would say, 'You sound different to me. Is there anything going on that you would like to talk about?' Sometimes a child isn't ready to talk about a problem to a parent, but will in a few days." There's a difference between a child who is simply having a bad day and one who is in extreme distress, and part of being a parent is recognizing that difference. If a student is often crying and sounds depressed, seeking help is in order. Knowing when and how to intervene is critical. Parents need to be able to distinguish when their child is not having a great day from when he is in crisis.

## Parents' Gut Feelings

If something is terribly wrong with their child, most parents can sense it in their child's voice and in their own visceral reaction, often described as "that feeling in the pit of your stomach." That is why the therapists with whom we talked agree that a voice on the phone at that point is better than a text or an email for conveying a student's emotional state.

Pam Matthews, an associate dean of the college of liberal arts at Texas A&M University, experienced a gut-wrenching reaction when her son called her in November of his freshman year, at 7 a.m. She knew immediately from his voice that something was horribly amiss. Barely able to talk, he was sitting outside his dorm room, unable to get up, get dressed, or go to class. Hundreds of miles away, Matthews knew that her only child was in trouble. As it turned out, these were the signs of a mood disorder that had surfaced suddenly and without warning that fall. Until that call Matthews and her husband knew nothing about it. She caught the first plane she could to rescue her son. In between flights she called her son, assuring him that she was on her way. She also alerted the college's dean and the counseling center. His friends stayed by his side until she arrived to take him back home.

Looking back, she realizes that the first hint of his illness emerged when they talked the night after dropping him off at his dorm. There was an unaccustomed note in his voice, "deader than panic, a listlessness, a lifelessness," she said. But her son had always done well at school and sailed easily through adolescence. There was no reason to think he wouldn't continue along the same successful arc. Reflecting on her experience, she wishes that she had known about the possibility of experiencing such a meltdown, even though the chances were slim. (About 11 percent of college students met criteria for a mood disorder, according to a recent study.) "Nobody saw this coming," Matthews said. "I never read anywhere in all the advice books, in all the get-ready-for-college books. Nobody said an awful lot of psychiatric illnesses have their onset in young adulthood. Although that might have scared me, boy, I would have appreciated knowing that. I'm not a psychologist. I would have liked some more well-rounded advice just to say chances are everything will be fine, but here are the stats."

Matthews's son is doing well now, but she has some hard-won words for parents of college students with mental health issues. First, she advises, in the first weeks of college, listen hard and insist on regular conversations with your child: "You don't have to be coercive, but you need to have an honest talk with them." Parents who have reason to be concerned might say, "I need you to be sensitive to the fact that I need to know you're okay. Indulge me." It doesn't have to be a thirty-minute dialogue; just a quick conversation will do. How much parents and children communicate is something that they need to work out together with their child's treating physician or therapist. That plan can be adjusted regularly to reflect the student's mental health needs.

## The Importance of Peers

While Matthews flew to rescue her son, his new college friends stayed by his side, and to them she is ever grateful. Shortly before that they had taken her son to the counseling center, and now they are still in touch with him, even though he is not at school. Their devotion and compassion show the important role that students' peers—roommates, friends, and teammates—can play in their lives, and parents will benefit from recognizing that. Matthews's case is not unique. Psychologists and psychiatrists repeatedly told us how supportive students' peers can be.

"It's been my experience that almost without exception there's a sports team or roommate or some other group that's involved and wanting to be helpful," said Ronald Albucher at Stanford. "That can be very therapeutic for the students with the problem. They won't be abandoned because they are different. Kids really normalize dealing with the illness, and the students are still part of the community."

The Active Minds organization builds on that strong compassion and the fact that students are sometimes more comfortable confiding in their peers. According to Alison K. Malmon, the founder and executive director of Active Minds, "Parents need to respect the wishes and needs of their child but also let them know that they are there for them. For kids now oftentimes they feel a lot more comfortable expressing emotions [typically to their peers] on a text, or a Facebook status. This is where students are comfortable with putting their emotions and feelings out there."

Malmon added, "Parents need to create allies and allegiances to help their student." For example, it's a good idea for parents to collect the phone numbers of their child's friends, using them only in a crisis situation. In fact this is a measure that won universal accord with our experts. Students can also be encouraged to be open about their problems with their trusted friends and share with them how to contact their parents. Malmon suggests they say, "If you get worried about me for any reason here's my parents' number."

## Advice to Parents

All parents need to educate themselves and their college-age children about mental health. It just makes good sense. Mental health is an issue that affects 57 million people in the United States each year, and a good number of these people are college students.

The best way parents can help their children is to open a supportive dialogue that invites communication. Be positive and genuinely interested in their lives. Listen carefully to what they say. Speak candidly and openly about mental illness.

## Chapter 10

# iConnecting after College

When Eric moved to Boston after graduating from college in upstate New York, he found it handy to have his mom ready to answer his daily (sometimes hourly) questions. Just a call away, whether from his new office, the apartment kitchen, or the corner laundry or grocery store, mom knew it all. Why bother to go elsewhere for advice or learn these things on his own when mom so loved these calls and the sense of being needed?

College offers preparation for adulthood, but whether students get that preparation depends not only on the college experience, but also on how parents interact with their children during those years. Students develop knowledge and expertise in a discipline and examine and redefine their identities. If all goes well, they learn to become genuinely intimate with others and to develop as independent individuals. Eventually they graduate and head out into the world, take up careers, and form lasting relationships. Parents hope that college has prepared their children for the adult world and that investment in a college education is an investment in a life, not just a credential. But sometimes parents are the ones who keep this from happening, however unintentionally.

## A Follow-up Study: Student-Parent Communication after Graduation

After learning about how students and parents communicated in the college years, we wanted to learn what happened in the years immediately after college. We wondered if their communication would change during this next transition into the work world, graduate school, or back home. Barbara and her thesis student Catherine Timmins sent another survey to Middlebury students who had participated in the first study, and who by now had graduated from college. Abby followed up with interviews of students and graduates from other colleges.

Even in the very recent past it seemed a sure thing that contact between parents and their recent college grads would have faded, overshadowed by the excitement of a new job, first apartment, and deeper romantic relationships. In the few years since Barbara and her students began studying student-parent communication, the expectation of being able to communicate with anyone, anywhere, and at anytime is now a way of life in the business world as well as academia. And parents, well, they are just as engaged as ever in their kids' lives.

The graduates in this follow-up study were communicating with parents even more out of college than during college. Now they were in touch 16.7 times per week, compared to the 13.4 times in their campus days. Just to make sure that this wasn't a reflection of an overall rise in everyone's level of communication, both in and out of college, we asked the students from the earlier study who were still enrolled in college (now juniors and seniors) to complete the survey. For them nothing had changed; they were communicating at the same rate as in the earlier study (13.4 times per week). So rather than diminishing in the years right after college, contact with parents appears to rise.

Among the graduates in the study, females were continuing to communicate more than males, averaging 17.9 contacts per week compared to 14.6 for males, not a large difference, and similar to the difference found in undergraduates. That means that guys aren't cutting the cord at any faster speed than their female counterparts. Parents still appear to be making more of the contacts (as reported by their kids), but now prefer email to cell phones, a departure from the college years. By contrast, young adults are still making more use of cell phone calls to link with the home front. Parents probably figure that with email they can reach out anytime, a bit less intrusively, and are more hesitant to interrupt work or social life with a call. On the other hand, the grads know their parents' more predictable schedules and when it works best to call them. Parents are also more likely to be reached on landlines in the home than are their kids. But overall both parents and grads were initiating more calls to each other than either group had done during college. Satisfaction with communication was still high, and most participants continued to want more contact with dads.

## Conversation Topics after College

Why are adult kids talking so much to their parents in these early years after college? "Because there's more to talk about now and more they can advise me about," said one grad, expressing a common response. Mom and dad can be quicker than Google to provide a recipe or advise how to fill out tax forms. Parents have a lifetime of experience on apartment security deposits and handling annoying coworkers, and many kids like tapping into it. As one grad recalled, "[We talked when] we were figuring out my new insurance policy. Or my apartment sublet situation."

Parents are also available for emotional support (as they are for decades, of course), and grads reported on how comforting this was. Even those who weren't regularly talking every day commented about particular times when the calls increased. "I called my mom more when I was having a really rough week, as many as 5–6 times per week during a string of awful days," wrote one survey respondent.

The transition from college to the working world is huge, as is the transition from high school to college. One recent college grad, Elizabeth, whom Abby interviewed, expanded on the challenges of this change. In the corporate world where she works as a campus relations specialist for a financial services company there are no more summer vacations, spring breaks, or the stimulation of different classes each semester. Appearances and first impressions count even more now, and young employees have to walk, talk, and dress the part. "Internships prepare you to a certain extent, and then you are in the workforce. There are those struggle points when things are a little uncertain and you look for comfort with your parents and want to know that things are going to be okay."

Other grads in the survey reported calling for the same reasons they did when they were in college: boredom and filling gaps of time between friends and work. Again the contrast with an earlier generation is striking. Not so long ago most young adults knew how to spend time on their own—and many still do, shooting hoops at a neighboring park or gym, taking a bike ride, listening to music, or reading a book. In a previous era, there were no cell phones or computers providing constant connection and entertainment. When young people were lonely or bored they reached out to a neighbor or a coworker, hoping to make a new friend. If they were upset or needed help they turned to friends, neighbors, or more experienced colleagues at work. Some young people just handled things on their own. In the end, though, most took charge of their life, learning in the process how to rely more deeply on themselves.

Today there are still some recent grads who rely less on parental advice than many of the students in our survey, either because they became more independent during their college years or are doing so now, learning to handle life on their own. To them the constant calls home that their friends are making can seem absurd and annoying.

There are positive aspects to these calls, however. Some graduates in the study commented on the increase in the mutuality of the conversations, more like friends talking to each other about each of their lives, a promising sign on the road to becoming an adult. Compared to their student years, some grads describe feeling more independent and appreciate being viewed as adults by their parents. They said that the conversations have become more open and closer, with greater "depth and significance." After college, parents and children often find themselves in flux as the child becomes more of an adult and the lines separating parent and child begin to fade.

Grads lucky enough to secure a job and some financial independence may now feel free from the obligation to constantly please their parents because they are no longer paying the bills. "In college I felt I had an obligation to be in constant touch, but I also enjoyed talking," recalled Molly, the student who felt conflicted about her constant contact with mom. Some of that obligation stemmed from her deep attachment to her mother and some from depending financially on her parents. "I resented that they leveraged my financial dependence to get me to do things that I didn't want to do. Little things, like I said when I was home 'I don't think I should have a curfew' and they said, 'Okay, give us back your credit card.' Now when my mother and I fight, she's at a loss because she doesn't have much left to leverage," she said, adding later, "It's a huge transition from college to where I am now, trying to figure out as an adult child how to relate to her parents."

## Parents Who Continue Offering Reminders

Our survey asked again about parents trying to run their kids' lives from afar. (Remember the parents who called to wake up their kids for class each day?) This had yet to decline. In fact results showed a continuing cycle of hypermanagement, stretching from high school (and no doubt before that), through college and now in the years after. Overall parents who nagged their kids in college to do their laundry, clean their room, and limit their drinking were still at it with these postcollege young adults.

These continued attempts to manage an adult child's life have the same unhappy consequences as they did in college. The grads that are least satisfied with their relationship with their parents are the ones who are still being hounded. Their relationships with mom and dad continue to be marked by control and conflict, evidenced in how they rated their relationships with parents. What is particularly troubling is that many of these individuals, trapped in a pattern of behavior spawned many years earlier, do not seem to have figured out a way to fix this problem. The very dependency their parents have engendered may keep them from challenging the relationship, and this is particularly true if the dependency is also financial. Parents need to recognize that if this is a familiar pattern, it is time to rethink this way of relating, give up some of their control, and begin to treat the growing adult as just that.

### Who Initiates the Contact, and Why This Matters
Again we found it matters considerably who is doing the initiating. Overall the grads in our survey say their parents initiate slightly more contact than they do, but the young adults who report the greatest satisfaction with their parents are those doing more of the initiating. They are most likely to rate their relationship with mom and dad as high in companionship. These are the grads who call their parents with the ups and downs of their days, much as they do with friends, and hear about their parents' lives as well. As one recent grad said, "I like my parents and truly enjoy talking with them and consider them my friends. They understand me and let me do my own thing, knowing that I freely reach out to them when I want to talk."

By contrast, the hovering parents are the ones who are doing much more of the calling and emailing. One who described this said, "My mom always bothers me about taking good care of myself. I tell her to quit it, and that I'm not a baby anymore." Many are less assertive, bothered by the impositions but relying on avoidance rather than confrontation.

The recent grads in this study report that they also dislike being asked what they are going to do next, after their current job or grad school. Even those who sought emotional support from parents really wanted just that—support—and were not asking their parents to solve their problems. One said, "When I am tired and lonely, my mom tries to give me a list of things to do which are overwhelming." The biggest conversational taboos in these early years after college, along with future plans, are sex and finances. Another unpopular topic: "Are you seeing anyone?"

Differences between the sexes persist in the subjects they discuss: "My dad and I talk about stocks and investments, and Mom gives me advice about relationships, being healthy. They both give me advice about work, the future, and living arrangements." Recommendations for action differ according to whether it's mom or dad talking: "My mom is more emotional, wants me to approach things somewhat spiritually or with a lot of internal reflection. My dad is more practical and hands-on." The financial crisis also looms in parental advice, but sometimes prompts conflicting messages: "My father suggests I look for a new job or grad school due to hours, low pay, and general dissatisfaction with my treatment [at my job], whereas my mother encourages me to stay in the current job due to the economy and unemployment rate."

### Emerging Adulthood and Life Satisfaction

We asked these recent grads to tell us how close they thought they were to adulthood. The good news is they saw themselves as closer to adulthood than they had in college. Some described this in detail: "I am more of a 'grown-up': I have a job and interact with older people in my everyday life. I think if anything I have matured and have refocused my priorities on the bigger picture, which in a way has made me feel closer to my parents." By contrast, those in a relationship with parents characterized as high in conflict were less likely to view themselves as adults. This was also the case for those still financially dependent on mom and dad, consistent with other research done on perceptions of adulthood.

The survey also asked them to rate their current *satisfaction with life*. This overall sense of well-being was tied to the perception of progress toward adulthood. They feel better about their postcollege lives if they feel they are now an adult or close to being one. Life satisfaction is also related to a positive relationship with parents and a sense of companionship with them. Those least satisfied with their lives are those whose relationships with their parents are difficult. Parents who think they are helping by continuing to manage their older children's lives might take note of this finding.

### Healthy Relationships in Emerging Adulthood

Clearly the relationship with parents continues to have a significant influence at this time of life. For most of those in our study, relationships with parents continue to be strong, and the characteristics are clear. Satisfying relationships with parents during this time of life are those low in conflict and control and high in companionship, comfort and understanding, and mutuality. Many of the graduates with whom we talked, as well as their parents, described their pleasure at finding these new adult relationships so satisfying.

At 24, Elizabeth now enjoys a close relationship with her parents, talking to or texting them nearly every day. She also prides herself on being independent and says her parents raised her that way, never nagging about her schoolwork, trusting her to get things done. Taking her current job at a financial services firm was her decision. "I like making decisions and taking charge of my future," she said. Now she lives two hours away from her parents but likes spending time with them. Indeed the day Abby talked to her she was heading off, happy to spend a long weekend in San Francisco with her parents to celebrate an uncle's fiftieth birthday.

## Emerging Adults in the Workplace: The View from College Career Counselors

Counselors in college career offices across the country can offer parents practical advice on how to help their students make the transition from school to work. These counselors are daily on the front lines of trying to manage the transition of this wave of superconnected college students, especially those who have been dependent on parental regulation or parental support, into the professional world.

At the University of Wisconsin at Whitewater families hear early on what employers are seeking in their newest recruits. "We say students have to stand on their own, to be independent," said Ron Buccholz, the university's director of career and leadership development, who addresses multiple groups of parents during the university's freshman orientation program. Much of his talk is devoted to explaining how parents can encourage their kids' steps toward independence. Doing so will help their kids find their passion and the skill sets that employers want. For example, parents can urge their kids to get involved in campus activities rather than just heading to the dorm when they aren't in class. Serving as a campus tour guide or helping plan activities on campus helps students develop organizational and personal communication skills. Studying abroad can also give kids the opportunity to be flexible and think on their feet. Employers value these experiences and skills. Other tips include urging students to write a résumé by their sophomore year;

this exercise visibly shows the gaps that students need to fill with an internship or other activities that pop off the page to prospective employers.

"Parents are shaking their heads and agreeing. After every session six, seven, or eight parents come up to me and say, 'I'm trying to do that,'" Buccholz said. Are parents really doing this? "I have no way of measuring that. But I do see evidence that some parents are out there trying to understand how they can support their children as they become independent and take charge of their lives."

At many other colleges career counselors begin working with parents and students during freshman orientation and continue cultivating their participation by helping students find jobs on campus, select a major, and apply for summer internships throughout their four years (or more) on campus. The biggest push, of course, starts junior year, when the prospect of finding a job or applying to graduate school moves closer to reality. It is also when most students have settled on a major and when counselors can help them identify which careers align with their majors. Parents are right on board. At Northwestern University parents are now the third most common referral source to the university's career services. "Some students say, 'My mother made me come.' We love to hear that. We see ourselves supporting parents," said Lonnie Dunlap, Northwestern's executive director of career services.

To a degree, that is. College career staff like Dunlap and Buccholz want parents to be engaged, but not overly so. A small and growing number of parents tend to lose sight of what's acceptable behavior. For example, a 2006 survey of college students by Experience Inc., a career services firm for college students and alumni, showed that 25 percent of students reported parents involved to the point of being "annoying or embarrassing" in their lives, including their job search efforts. The company's CEO, Jenny Floren, says she has seen no signs of parental hovering letting up.

211

Just as they influence their children's college majors, parents shape their career choices, according to interviews with career counselors, employers, and young job seekers. College career counselors find themselves trying to manage parents' expectations that a particular major and degree will lead to a specific career. Parents do wield clout—at last as far as their children's goals. In another Experience survey 60 percent of students and alumni reported that role models helped influence their career paths. Who were the top two role models? Teachers or professors (46 percent) and parents (41 percent).

## A Bad Economy Increases Parents' Anxiety and Involvement

The troubled economy is raising the tide of parental involvement. "There are very few people working today in the United States who have great confidence that the organization in which they are working, and their role in that organization, are stable," said William Wright-Swadel, executive director of Duke University's career services. Parents feel an enormous sense of urgency in their children's finding a major that will lead to a secure career and guarantee lifelong employment, an unrealistic expectation for the child and the career. Economic forecasters have noted that workers should be prepared to change jobs as well as careers several times during their lifetime. "There is nothing that says a twenty-two-year-old should know the career that they are going to retire on," Wright-Swadel said. This understandable quest for security by parents often makes matters worse for their kids. "What they're doing is creating a sense of urgency that doesn't allow students the time to explore and to find the field or the passion or the skill sets that they are going to be most reliant upon. Focus and decision are born out of exploration and discovery, not urgency."

Wright-Swadel often uses humor to help parents gain some perspective when he sees them pushing a child down a career path that isn't the best fit for her, and he does it early on. Known for its top-notch medical school, Duke often attracts students who think—or whose parents think—that they would make great doctors. Once students begin taking the demanding premed courses, however, some change their minds, to their family's dismay. "I tease the parents that if they need a physician in the family and if they leave the child alone to make their own decision, I'll help one of the *parents* go to medical school." The joke, he said, is simply a way to get the parents to realize that this transition is not just for individual students but for parents too. But behind the humor is a frustration and worry shared by other career counselors and articulated by Wright-Swadel: "Where is the explosive growth and discovery of passion going to come from if parents are going to drive the decisions? When does the student acquire the adult behavior of learning how to manage a career, life, and a family?"

Some career counselors find themselves caught in the middle, between parents and students. Many tell of parents who call them, asking for help in dissuading their children from career choices. Those to whom we talked decline to dissuade the students, suggesting that parents discuss the issue themselves with their kids. On the flip side, career counselors often work with students, even role-playing, to help them tell parents about any changes in their plans.

## Levels of Parental Involvement in Students' Career Search

Involved parents today are taking an active part in their child's career search. Some are helping in fairly normal ways, proofreading résumés and cover letters and leveraging any job connections they might have.

The survey study showed that about 33 percent of parents proofread résumés and about 25 percent look over their child's cover letters.

Other parents are being far more aggressive, actually writing the résumés and cover letters, scoping out recruiters at campus career fairs and making sure their kids meet them, scheduling interviews at staffing agencies, and even accompanying students on job interviews. Some young job seekers see this behavior as detrimental. "If I'm applying for jobs and my mom contacted the employers, they would be taken aback by it," said Marcus, a recent graduate from the University of Minnesota, still actively searching for a job in communications. A good number of college career advisors say these actions are over the top and harmful to the kids' jobs search. At Experience, Jenny Floren reports that some parents log in to their kids' accounts, fill out job applications, and sign them up for job interviews. That's "way over the line," said Floren, who gently tries to discourage parents from overinvolvement. "It is one thing to be a coach and another thing to be a body double."

Lonnie Dunlap told us about one bank that regularly recruits at Northwestern, whose recruiter called a couple of years ago about a father who had overstepped his bounds. His son had interviewed for a desirable position at the bank, and the father, impatient with the process, took it upon himself to call the bank to see where his son stood. His son didn't get the job. Whether he would have made the final cut isn't known, but that dad's call took his child out of the running, said Dunlap.

Northwestern now tries to head off such behavior by sharing similar stories with parents during freshman orientation. Dunlap goes one better by asking parents in the audience who also are employers to offer advice on what parents should and shouldn't do to help their children find a job. The employers, especially the younger ones, understand how much parents want to be involved, she said. What employers appreciate most is the support that parents provide, but not the interference. Support your children behind the scenes, encouraging them in their search and interviews, but don't call the employer yourself.

*What Parents Can Do to Support Their Child's Job Search*
Career counselors with whom we talked said parents can encourage their students to use their school's career services, but should not carry out the job search for them. For starters, students can write their own résumés, cover letters, and follow-up thank-you notes to the people who interviewed them. Students may review their résumé with their parents, but the student needs to write it. "It builds skills for students to do all aspects of a job search. It's a lifelong skill for their own career management," said Dunlap. "They should also do their own research on the employer and the work setting, so it's in their head when they go to interview and they can use it during the interview."

Parents can also help prepare their kids for interviews by coaching them on the kinds of questions that employers are likely to ask, said Jill Evans Silman, vice president of Meador Staffing Services in Shenandoah, Texas, which places people in temporary and permanent positions in a range of industries, regionally and nationally. For example, she said, parents can role-play with their child. A typical question: "What are the skills and experience that make you the best person for the job?" To stay in the running a candidate should be able to deliver a brief and compelling summary, matching his or her skills to the position's requirements.

Parents, though, have to be careful not to let their own financial concerns shine through during the interview. Asking about the company's benefits should not be the third question out of an applicant's mouth; it often signals a planted concern of parents. "Sometimes I'll get a question [from a job applicant] and I can tell that they don't even know what they are asking," said Silman. For example, applicants applying for a temporary position will ask about vesting, even though they are not even going to be there longer than six months, she said.

## Employers Want Decision Makers, but Aren't Always Getting Them

Ironically the rising tide of parental involvement is nurturing qualities in kids that are exactly the opposite of what employers want. A 2009 survey by the National Association of Colleges and Employers listed the most desirable skills for young job candidates; initiative and communication skills are among the most prized. If mom and dad consistently do the talking and decision making for their kids, their kids aren't likely to develop those skills. And employers are experiencing the fallout from these well-meaning moms and dads. In interviews with employers large and small, they told us about new hires that were unable to make decisions on their own and solve problems promptly.

Brett Good is district president for southern California and Arizona for Robert Half International, one of the world's largest specialized staffing firms. He personally looks for candidates who possess initiative, self-reliance, and the ability to think quickly on their feet. Whether those candidates service clients within the Robert Half company or work with their external clients, those traits are essential, especially in the current economy. "When you look at organizations that have cut so deeply into management, there's not a lot of handholding that can take place. Problems need to be solved very quickly," Good said. But in the ten years he has worked recruiting entry-level employees he has noted a gradual change in their attributes that has accelerated over the past few years.

"Today you still have very great and capable graduates coming in, very skilled and very technically savvy. But there seems to be a growing schism between those that feel able and empowered to make decisions independently and those that are deferring decisions to more committees or checking in to ask their peers or their network before making the decision," he said. Sometimes parents are part of that network, said Good, who gleans this information from one-on-one meetings with young employees in which they discuss their decisions and who their coaches and mentors are. Young adults just entering the workforce need a little time to find a work mentor, and until they do it's understandable that they would consult a parent with work experience about job issues. Nonetheless, Good said, "I hear that parents are part of that network, mentoring, and coaching group more times today than I did ten years ago."

That tendency to consult, he said, "slows down the process and can put their careers at risk, if they lose clients or slow down the process internally for other clients. Their decisions are part of a chain of decisions that need to be made." These types of decisions are not monumental: "These are smaller decisions that newer employees should be able to make." Unfortunately our economy has little tolerance for these kinds of inefficiencies, he said. Employees who don't have the requisite decision-making skills are likely to be terminated.

Enterprise Rent-A-Car is seeing some of the same issues. "At Enterprise, we're very entrepreneurial," said Angela Kundert, a recruiting manager for the company. "We want them to treat this like they are running their own business," she said, referring to the company's new management trainees. For some of these young employees, that's been a bit of a challenge. The management trainee learns on the job with a branch manager and also receives other training for several months. "Some of the challenges are that a customer comes in and is upset. We want the employee to make [the problem] go away, to make that customer happy. Some employees are not comfortable making that call on their own, even if they are making the right decision. Instead they go to their manager." Enterprise, which hires eight thousand management trainees annually, tries to counter this pattern by encouraging its young trainees to come up with their own solutions, she said. To illustrate her point, she described this scenario in an email: Young trainees frequently pick up customers at body shops or service shops to bring them back to the branch to pick up their rental car. Sometimes, when they arrive at the branch, the customer and trainee learn that the customer's driver's license has expired. Some management trainees may think they need a manager's approval or "blessing" and so ask the manager how to proceed; however, one trainee thought quickly and decided to take the customer to the nearest DMV and wait while his license was renewed. "This example was a situation where it was an honest mistake on the part of the customer, and it was easily resolved by our management trainee just taking a little extra time to go above and beyond and win the loyalty of that customer."

In an email Kundert wrote, "I'm not sure everyone would have handled it the same way. However, as part of the overall management training program, we encourage autonomy and a think-on-your-feet type of work style. Today's generation isn't always as geared toward that style at first, but as they go through our program they are more likely to develop a sense of autonomy for decision-making, rather than the need to consult with a manager on day-to-day type decisions." Kundert traces part of the problem to the dependent way many of these young employees have been raised: they are not used to making decisions on their own.

*Employers' Reactions to Parents at Job Fairs and Interviews*
Mom and dad have emerged as presences in the workplace in ways unimaginable even a few years ago. A few parents are pushing the limits. Company recruiters now report seeing parents with their students at career fairs, which didn't happen a few years back. "The parents are cheerleaders, saying 'Go talk to that company,' pointing at

the booths. Or parents physically come up to the booth themselves," said Tammy A. McCormack, human resources director at PKWARE, Inc., an international security software provider based in Madison, Wisconsin. As a policy, McCormack is always polite to parents approaching her booth. When a parent arrives with his or her child, she talks to both. But if a parent is alone and wants to pass along the child's résumé because the child is elsewhere at the fair, McCormack refuses to take it. Instead she asks the parent nicely to please have the child do it—making the point that it's the child's responsibility to take this first step in the job search. When mom and dad take such an active role in their adult child's job search, McCormack and other human resources recruiters wonder, "Do they have the confidence to do this on their own?"

Elizabeth shared a similar reaction when she recently saw a mom accompanying a student at a campus career fair. Elizabeth is only a few years older than the students at the fair, yet she said, "I thought it was inappropriate. At that age, they should be making decisions and have the professionalism to handle events alone. . . . It just shows they lack maturity, and I question whether they will make decisions on their own."

Parents also have been spotted taking their children to actual job interviews. In her previous human resources position at a prestigious law firm in Milwaukee, McCormack met on separate occasions two mothers arriving with their sons for day-long interviews for coveted summer associate positions. Both men were in their second year of law school. "I was shocked," she said. She tried to give some gentle guidance to the mothers, telling them, "I have to be honest. We are very traditional here. It might be nice not to accompany him." She then directed the mothers to a nearby mall and museum for the day. If any of the partners had gotten wind of the moms that would have spelled an immediate rejection for the two young men. As it turned out, no one saw them, but the young men didn't get hired anyway, she said.

Parents who accompany their children to a job fair or job interview immediately raise a red flag about their child's maturity and ability to function independently. "Oh, my god, I would think twice about hiring them," said Kristine Sabat, senior vice president of production at KPI, a television production company based in Manhattan. KPI crews film all over the world to produce programs for broadcast outlets such as MSNBC and the History and Discovery channels. "The people we hire have to be very self-sufficient and proactive!" On a film shoot, she said, "they have to be aware of what's coming up next and what they are going to have to do and think ahead. They have to make things happen on their own."

### Parental Involvement in the Job Offer

Once the interviews are over, many parents play a part when job offers are made. Even in today's employment-scarce economy, many recent college graduates and those just a few years older will not respond to a job offer until they discuss it first with their parents. At Robert Half International, Brett Good said, "Typically I will hear, 'Thank you for this offer. I want to run this by my mentors and advisors.'" About 40 percent of the time, he said, they ask their parents for advice. This occurs not only with students seeking parental input on a first real job; it happens with young candidates on their second or third job. The same scenario plays out at Enterprise. "It's the last three to four years that I've seen people wanting to talk things over with mom and dad," said Angela Kundert. "Ten years ago, I couldn't tell you that I ever heard of that. Now, I would say seventy-five percent take the job offer right off the bat, but some want to think about it, and a quarter of that number will say they want to talk to mom and dad." Even when it comes to accepting a temporary job, some candidates say they have to run it by mom and dad first, said Jill Silman of Meador.

Although this behavior does not set off the alarm bells that a parent tagging along on a job interview does, it may not be the image that a soon-to-be professional wants to project. For example, at Rice University advisors at the center for student professional development try to discourage students from making such admissions to employers. They ask students to consider how their need to seek parental approval will make them appear to their potential employer. When hearing it put that way, students laugh, said Jackie Hing, the center's associate director. "Even if a student does talk to their parent, there is a part of that same student that wants to be independent." Now they just need to *become* independent.

No doubt about it, accepting a first job is an exciting and sometimes complicated event. For some the job comes with a benefits package, a compensation plan, and a bundle of information that is new to most recent college grads. Today some new employees ask their employers to send copies of those benefits packages to their parents for review. At Enterprise, a firm known for embracing this superconnected wave of young employees, it is not even an unusual request.

### How Parents Can Support Their Children at Their New Job

A 2006 watershed survey of more than four hundred human resources and senior managers in a wide range of companies identified key skills that new young entrants to the workforce are lacking. Among them are professionalism, a work ethic, the ability to work as a team, oral communication, critical thinking, and problem-solving skills, said Mary Wright, program director for The Conference Board, which sponsored the survey along with Corporate Voices for Working Families, the Partnership for 21st Century Skills, and the Society for Human Resource Management. The survey's findings are a blueprint for parents on how to assist their kids in their careers. Meador's Jill Silman agrees: "More than anything, parents can encourage a good work ethic, attendance, punctuality, honesty, and commitment. These are the things that employers are looking for."

221

About a decade ago Texas employers were asked to name the two most important employee qualities, she said. "The first was to be at work every day, and the second was to be at work every day on time." These behaviors may seem simple and self-evident to people already in the workforce, but for some students who have never had a full-time job or have an elastic definition of punctuality, they are worth noting.

In some instances, Silman has had parents calling in to excuse their kids, as they did in their child's school years. Although well-meaning, this kind of parental intervention prevents a young employee from being seen as professional and from moving up the ladder professionally. It also delays his growth toward adulthood.

Human resource professionals and career counselors say parents can support their children in their new job by helping them understand their employer's management structure and what constitutes professional behavior. A number of employers say some young employees don't recognize or understand typical management boundaries. Parents can compensate for this gap by explaining why it's important not to go over their boss's head or correct their boss publicly. Parents who are experienced in the work world can help by explaining office politics and why it's important to get along with coworkers. If their child receives an unsatisfactory performance review, parents can ask her to examine honestly whether she deserved that review, and what she can do to improve her performance. Young employees need to develop the ability to solve problems; if they rely on parents for constant advice, they won't develop that skill.

Parents also do well by their children by urging them to find a mentor at their workplace. "Talking to parents is good. But from my own personal experience the best thing you can do is to find a mentor within that organization. There are many nuances in an organizational culture and you'll never pick up on a good many of them without a mentor," Mary Wright said.

*Moms on Business Trips, at Company Parties, and in
Office Cubicles*

Some companies have found parents playing an unprecedented role in the workplace. One recent college grad at PKWARE, Inc., took her mother along to a business conference in San Francisco. Other employees were taking spouses on the trip, which prompted her to make the request; this shocked Tammy McCormack, the firm's human resources director. "I don't think I would do that," she said. Still, she said she admired the young woman for asking permission and sensing that taking her mom along might raise some eyebrows. McCormack and company officials decided to treat the mom as if she were a spouse, allowing her to stay at no cost in her daughter's hotel room, but required her to pay for her own plane ticket and meals. The mother-daughter pair stayed on after the conference, making it a long weekend.

Parents also are popping up as their children's guests at PKWARE's company parties in the winter and summer, McCormack said. The other employees react to the new guests just fine. "They say, 'We have heard about you,' which kind of makes me feel guilty since I never invited my mom. It's usually the mom, nine times out of ten." The practice is still unconventional, however. At a recent holiday party at the company's Dayton, Ohio, office, one young woman teasingly introduced her mother as her date, drawing snickers from some of her coworkers, McCormack said. At Meador's company picnics and barbecues, young female employees have arrived with their mothers. "They said, 'You told me I could bring somebody.' I just assumed it was going to be a spouse," said Silman.

Emails, calls, texts, even social networking between parents and their working children are becoming part of the work culture. Brooke Carlson, vice president of business development for CONAIR, Inc., in Stamford, Connecticut, has a number of young employees under her watch. "Now when you walk into someone's office, you'll hear,

'I'll have to call you back, dad, mom,'" she said, noting that she rarely heard those sign-offs four years ago. Tammy McCormack also reports that, after several warnings, she had to discipline one young man for being on Facebook too many times on the job. In his defense he said he was talking to his mother.

It's also not uncommon for parents to visit their children's workplace. Rebecca recently invited her mom to visit her office to share her new work experience, in which she is now thriving: "I really wanted her to see my office, where I eat lunch, and see my coworkers." Some coworkers found it a little "funny," said Rebecca. One in particular, who teases Rebecca for her innocence and enthusiasm, reportedly said, " 'Bambi' is bringing her parents to work." "I said, 'Yeah, I am bringing them and I'm proud of it.'"

## A Cultural Divide on Parents' Role in the Workplace

A generational and perhaps cultural divide is emerging on what's considered an acceptable level of parental involvement in the workplace. Some employers, such as Enterprise and PKWARE, are more accepting. Observes Tammy McCormack, "We're a securities software company. The average age here is forty-two. We're young. We're hip. We're happening. And because of that culture, we're more open in that way."

But in some workplaces, even where family calls from children, spouses, and parents are a part of life, there's a limit. Molly works in close quarters, and her coworkers and boss often heard her mother's frequent calls during her first weeks on the job. To give her mother the hint, Molly would answer a call with, "Mom, *again*?" and would hear them laughing in the background. (Molly said her mom immediately picked up on the cue, afraid she was jeopardizing her daughter's career.)

Some employers are decidedly not as accepting, especially those in high-pressure industries that place a premium on independence and initiative. Barry Frank is executive vice president of Media Sports

Programming at IMG, one of the world's most prominent media, entertainment, and sports enterprises. He has mentored a number of well-known sports figures and has strong feelings about what attributes he seeks in his interns and youngest employees: "I want someone who can stand on their own two feet without telling them what to do. I want to see what they can do. They've been to three or four years of college. Show me what you can do." Frank thinks it's smart for inexperienced employees to check in with parents on issues such as how much to contribute to a 401(k) plan, but not on specific work decisions. Parents can also act as mentors to their children, as he did with his own children. But helping children make on-the-job decisions—that leaves Frank puzzled, among other things. "I can't figure out where that would work," he said, pausing before poking fun at the concept with an example of an airline pilot asking his parents, "Is it too cloudy to fly today?" As for bringing mom to a holiday party or on a business trip, Frank found such parental involvement "appalling," viewing it as a step backward in a young employee's development and an indication of not being able to separate appropriately from her family.

Sometimes the parental imprint is less visible but more powerful. At Enterprise parents have also talked directly to the company about plans to relocate their child. Over at her company, Elizabeth discusses with young talent various opportunities throughout the company. Often the younger employees will tell her they want to think about it first. "Then they come back and will say, 'I talked to my parents and they think . . . ' A lot of conversations begin that way. I don't know whether they are making decisions on their own or whether it's the parent talking." Elizabeth is a bit frustrated with the situation. "The big thing is to trust the kid and let go. Sometimes I want to call parents and say, 'You raised your kid. You put the work in. Now you have to let them go and trust that you did a good job and trust them that they will make a good decision.'"

225

## Advice to Parents

The patterns of behavior between parents and students in college, and likely before that in high school, persist in the years after college. Postgrads who take the lead in contacting their parents are more likely to have a satisfying relationship with them than their peers whose parents are doing more of the calling, texting, and emailing. Not surprisingly these young people are also more likely to feel better about themselves if they see themselves as moving toward adulthood—which is harder to do if mom and dad are constantly phoning in advice and direction.

When it comes to assisting their children with the search for a job, parents need to think of what will best suit their kids and not what pleases themselves. This may be a little hard for mom and dad to swallow when they are expecting a financially secure career in exchange for a big tuition fee. But in the end, it is the child who will have to go to work each day and build a life around a chosen career, so being the one to choose that work is critically important for his or her well-being.

Parents also need to support their child's search for a career in ways that will foster self-reliance, a trait prized by employers. Assisting a child in preparing a résumé might be acceptable, but writing it for him is not. Similarly young job seekers need to take charge of all the elements in a job search; it's a skill that will serve them well in the future. Helping a child figure out a contribution to a 401(k) plan at her new job makes a lot of sense, but trying to renegotiate her salary does not; it's overstepping, and employers will resent it. When their children secure a job—a real milestone today—parents need to be mindful of how they can positively support them. Once again this means encouraging children to take responsibility for their behavior on the job, learning about their company's culture, being reliable, and developing a mentor relationship in their workplace.

## Advice for Companies

Companies today find themselves in the middle of a cultural shift, trying to adjust to a wave of young employees superconnected to their parents. While these young employees bring a wealth of talent, some bring less desirable traits, bred by too much dependence on mom and dad and the temptation of a touch screen cell phone. As companies know, managers can help modify those behaviors by clearly encouraging their new employees (and not their parents) to take full responsibility for their jobs: coming to work on time, learning how to behave in a work environment, developing appropriate relationships with their peers and supervisors. Employees' parents who know that's what is expected are also likely to help their children have more success on the job.

## Chapter 11

# How Parents Can Stay Close but Let Their Kids Grow Up

Parents, educators, and employers have reason to be concerned about the findings of our research and reporting, as do young people. Some college students are talking to their parents so much or are so accustomed to hypermanaging parents that they are stuck developmentally, unable to move on to the next, natural steps in their lives. Many college students aren't doing their own work or managing their own lives on campus, or after they graduate. As young employees they are jeopardizing their jobs and their companies because they can't make a decision on their own or don't know that it may be inappropriate to bring mom to a company function. This is not happening in every family, but the trend is seeping into our culture, influencing parenting practices and how families communicate and interact in the larger world.

It takes deliberate attention to manage technology in order to parent in positive ways. Learning to do this effectively takes forethought and planning, so that you have a satisfying relationship with your adult children and so that they become healthy and independent and can take care of themselves and be responsible to others.

Learning to use cell phones as a parenting tool requires the same self-discipline as managing email overload. You enhance your productivity by not treating every email as an interruption. Turn off the pinging sounds, focus on your work, and check email only at set times. Of course we adults don't always manage email effectively, but you can identify principles for managing technology that also apply to connecting with your growing children. When we're asked why parents are talking to their kids so much, we've found the simplest answer to be "Because they can." This doesn't mean that they *should*, however, and learning to be more mindful about these connections can enhance your child's development as well as enrich your relationship with this emerging adult. Focus consciously on when, why, how, and what you're communicating with your children. Ask yourself: Do I need to make this call now? Am I making this call for my benefit or for my child's benefit? Is what I need to say best conveyed by phone, or in an email, or in a simple text message? Is there a way to convey my message in ways that are not controlling?

As our research and reporting show, too much parental contact that is overly controlling (whether intended or not) is not good for a child at any age, but especially not for one on the threshold of adulthood. You may be thwarting your child's development. Yet given the ease of communication, it can be difficult for parents to change their behaviors when kids start college. Not so long ago kids struggled through the transitions of those early weeks at college without talking about every detail with their parents, and if they had problems they summarized them in the Sunday-night call, typically after the problems had been at least somewhat resolved or the emotional heat had faded. Maybe the roommate problem was discussed with another new friend, or the stinging comments on a first piece of writing were soothed by realizing in a conversation over lunch that these were actually helpful criticisms. Little of this was channeled into phone calls home.

Now parents and kids can talk every day. But should they? How can parents handle this desire for communication and the need to let go? What's in the best interests of the kids? Sometimes it's too easy for parents to phone out of their own need for reassurance, and this is not good for an emerging adult. Similarly kids may call home for comfort they could be learning to seek elsewhere or provide for themselves, or for help solving problems they could learn to solve on their own, which can be especially hard for parents to deflect and redirect. Our advice is based on the results of our own research and reporting as well as broader psychological research and wisdom. The challenge of this period of life is to remain close and connected while giving college students the space they need to mature.

## Start Early

At an orientation session for parents on the topic of fostering autonomy, one parent said that he was most grateful to get the information not just for the son beginning college that week, but also for the son still at home. He realized how important it is to start preparing his younger son.

If you are reading this as a high school parent, consider *now* how to begin preparing your child for the independence of college. Sometimes this takes only small steps, handing off simple chores like laundry or making sure he or she can get off to school without your help, tasks that children can master long before leaving home, but sometimes don't. Larger issues include learning to manage money and becoming the kind of student who is on top of assignments or tries very hard to be.

Parents who have been successful in this regard have offered tips. Sally, mother of Sam, whom we profiled in an earlier chapter, said she used sports to instill self-reliance in her sons: "We tried to have them be independent from early times. With sports we encouraged them how to figure out how to get their own equipment and to figure out their practice schedule."

When it comes time to apply for college, be a thorough sounding board for your child and provide relevant information that will help guide the decision process; for example, teach them the significance of financial aid. Make sure your son or daughter is doing as much of the work as possible on his or her own, soliciting information, making contacts with schools, arranging interviews, creating checklists with due dates. Each small step increases your child's ownership of the process and deepens his or her personal investment in the college experience. You might plan a trip together to schools of interest, but when you're back in the car avoid offering your own judgment until after your child shares his or her perceptions. When other parents ask you where your child is applying, or you speak to a college admissions officer, it is wise to avoid the use of the word "we" when you respond. Few verbal slips are more telling.

When Sam applied for college he knew that he would do best in a college with small classes, where he could develop relationships with professors. He also knew his ability in sports might win him a spot on a team, creating another supportive community for him. He made these decisions in consultation with his parents, but they were *his* decisions. Sam's first choice was a college across the country from his home on the West Coast. His dad knew it would be Sam's first choice when he saw how his son reacted so positively during their visit, but his mother worried about the distance and how he would handle college along with his ADHD. Having his brother and cousins in a nearby city helped take the edge off his mother's anxiety.

## Before College: Decide Together How Often to Talk

Before your child leaves for college discuss how often he might want to communicate. Then surrender as much control of that interaction as you can, while striving for some common ground. If your child is already in college and you haven't had this conversation, have one now. You might be surprised. Opening these avenues of communication, talking explicitly about your own communication, is a healthy step toward creating an adult relationship with your teenager. You might also consider assuring him that there is no need to talk every day, even if others are doing it, because you want to make sure to provide room for independence. At the end of the first semester talk about how your communication patterns are working for both of you.

## Set a Regular Time to Talk

Savor the spontaneity that arises with the easy access of cell phones and enjoy the quick calls from your kids that provide a window on their experience. ("We just finished practice and coach says I'm starting in the game on Saturday!") Who doesn't love sharing in that moment? But also find a time that works for both of you to catch up, when you can have that longer call and share in the details of her life that she wants to disclose and when you can offer news from home. In between be careful about *when* you initiate calls. One mom reported her embarrassment at calling her daughter and catching her at a party during the first year of college. The daughter answered promptly, fearing that a Friday-night call might mean something was wrong at home. She couldn't believe her mom was calling just to chat (and perhaps was not too confident about wanting to talk to her mom while in party mode). The daughter's disbelief and reluctance to talk were very clear. Her mom learned the hard way that too much spontaneity can be a problem.

Sam's mom said that he and his older brother were ready to be independent when they went off to college. "They would say, 'Get a life, mom!' . . . If I was asking too many questions via email, they would choose not to respond or would answer when they were ready." She missed her sons, but recognized that each needed to separate and start his own life.

## Monitor the Early Months, but with Deliberate Caution

The early months of college can be volatile, tumultuous, and tremendously exciting. This is a good time to be particularly attentive to emotional cues. But don't overdo the checking in, as you're also establishing a pattern here. Savor your child's excitement and your ability to hear the ups and downs, but don't ask for that to be a daily practice or imply that you expect it. For example, avoid saying "I didn't hear from you yesterday. Is everything okay?" This is also a good time to ask for a roommate's cell phone number as an emergency backup. Make it clear what those situations might be, such as letting your child know about unexpected travel plans or an accident or illness in the family, and only when use of other channels has failed to get a response. Students we've talked with assure us that not having heard from a kid in two days when everything otherwise seems normal does not qualify!

## Be Mindful of Who's Initiating Communications

Our research is clear that when college students are the ones initiating slightly more of the calls they feel stronger about their relationship with their parents. This element of feeling in control and making choices about when to initiate communication is crucial to their healthy development of independence. Conversely, those in our study who reported that their parents were the ones doing most of the calling were least happy with their relationship with their parents.

This doesn't mean you should *not* call. But try not to make all or most of the calls, and create a conversational style that prompts your child to want to call you. (More on that later.) Strive for balance. When you have an urge to reach out to your child, consider whose needs would be met by that contact. If they are primarily yours, consider waiting and giving your child a chance to initiate. If he expects you to call constantly, he may be less likely to reach out on his own, and taking that initiative is important.

Sam's dad reported that, as Sam has progressed through his years at college, he has become reengaged with his parents, calling them two or three times a week. "I think he likes to stay connected at various times," his dad said. "He'll call on the landline and [leave a message]: 'Okay, family, where are you? I'm trying to talk with you!'" Or if he plays well on his team, his dad said, "He'll call and say, 'Look at the [school] website.'" Occasionally his parents have flown out to see him play, and Sam has welcomed them happily.

## Include Dads

One of the most robust findings across our set of studies is the desire that many students, especially daughters, have for more connection with their dad. Cell phones make it easier for a call to be person-to-person rather than from kid to home, with both parents in on the call. Because mom seems to be getting more of the calls, some dads may be getting left out. To moms we recommend trying hard to include dads in the communication. Again, a weekly scheduled call provides more opportunity for both parents in two-parent households to be available for the conversation (whether it's simultaneous or sequential), with one-to-one calls in between. If parents are not living together, each parent may want to think about how to engage directly.

We encourage dads not only to reach out and initiate more contact, but also to make it clear you're available if your child wants to call you. Do let her know that you welcome her calls. Set parameters, if needed, around the best times to call. Find a medium that works for you for easy exchange (for some dads that's quick texting), but also consider how you can make an occasional phone call. It will be appreciated, as we have learned from students in our studies and interviews.

## Use Email Too—and Don't Forget "Care Packages"

When you want to say something that you think would be better to have your child read and think about before discussing it with you an email is more productive than a phone call. ("We're thinking we might want to visit you next weekend, but want to make sure this would be convenient for you.") It can also be a good way for your child to float an idea to you. ("I'm considering going to New Zealand to study abroad.") Email is also great for quick connections, such as sending a photo from home, a news clip from the local papers, a forwarded note from a relative. A good number of students talked about how their dad made these types of connections through email, often forwarding some piece in the news that he knew was of mutual interest. The students were touched by these gestures. Even if dad isn't likely to be calling often, emailing is a means for him to stay in touch and let his children know that he is thinking of them.

Students still love getting the occasional card or letter, and these have taken on more significance in the age of easy calling. The well-timed care package with cookies from home is always appreciated. Don't let cell phone calls replace other means of connecting just because calling is so easy.

## Give Them Space to Lead Their Own Lives, and Know the Boundaries

College students need to have their own lives, and they need enough emotional space to navigate them themselves. It can be tempting to want to know everything and to continue to be a part of their lives the way you might have been in high school. Their lives are so much more exciting now. But part of going to college is learning where to set boundaries around privacy. Maybe your son wants to wait and see how a relationship develops before he talks about it with you. Sharing the crush stage with a new roommate first, instead of with a parent, is a healthy step toward building new friendships and trust. Those who have to process it all with parents first may still be struggling with emotional autonomy.

Most students are likely to be pretty clear about what they want to talk about and what they don't. We have learned that they have figured out some ways of protecting their boundaries, although they aren't always direct or even honest in the process. The ideal is to help kids draw boundaries in ways that are respectful of their privacy yet still promote health and safety. It probably isn't useful to ask how much she had to drink or to insist that she never drink, but making her aware of research on binge drinking might be productive, although these are conversations that might best take place before college and during breaks, face to face.

One of our research participants talked about her mom as a "Chatty Cathy" who needed to be talking with her all the time. Several students described a level of invasiveness in parental questioning. This can be oppressive. Do make it clear that you're interested in hearing about what he's doing, but let him decide how much to offer up.

Respect your child's boundaries. We recommend that you don't initiate a Facebook "friend request" to kids who are in college. This is their own social network and a place to experiment with identity. Let them decide whom they wish to include. Later, after college, when they are in the work world, they may be more interested in connecting with you in this way. By that time most individuals have learned about the public nature of social media and are generally more cautious about what they display. If you're visiting campus on parents' weekend, skip the beer pong. Colleges are filled with embarrassing stories of parents trying too hard to be a part of their child's new life.

## Know How to Respond to Venting

It can be especially helpful to remember that sometimes when college students call home and complain, they are just venting to a receptive audience, not asking for help. Don't interpret each complaint as a need to soothe or intervene. It's easy to get caught up in your child's panic ("I'm not at all prepared for this test and I'm sure I'm going to blow it!"), irritation ("My roommate is so messy and we're never going to be friends"), or complaints ("The dining hall hours suck"). Remember that going to college requires adjustments on his part and that learning to adapt is part of his growth during these years. He needs to learn how to solve problems for himself. Step back, take a deep breath, let him talk, but don't rush in to fix it.

This isn't always easy, we know, and the emotional intensity of such calls can be hard on parents. A set of parents in an orientation session told the group that it took them a while to learn that they became much more riled up by their daughter's calls than was necessary. They realized over time that she was usually calling just to vent, not crying for help. She would unload and then feel better afterward, but at the end of those heated conversations the parents often felt anxious and upset, having absorbed the emotional turmoil of the call and transformed it into parental worry. In their solicitous follow-up calls she hardly remembered what she had told them, which was a rude shock to parents who had spent a sleepless night. Their solution was to resist answering most of her daytime calls, knowing that she'd leave a message if it were really urgent, and calling her back later. This strategy has been successful; now they talk to her after her moods have leveled off, which is better for all of them. Other parents might be more willing to take the heat, recognizing it for what it is, but they might want to let the emerging adult know that he or she can begin to develop other strategies besides unloading on parents all the time.

It can be difficult to talk about something you're not thrilled to hear about. (Imagine the kid who calls and says, "I'm so excited! We're going to drive up to Montreal for the weekend, where the drinking age is eighteen!") Sam's parents said, "It puts a bigger burden on parents now to say 'no.' Before, a kid wouldn't be able to get to you. Now they can get to you and you get sucked into their life a lot more easily. The technology has made parenting in that sense harder."

*Practice Good Listening*
Many parents took classes when their kids were young about "how to talk so your kids will listen and listen so your kids will talk." Seldom is this listening as important as during the college years, when face-to-face interactions are so limited and cell phone conversations are the bulk of the connection. But there isn't much available in the way of a refresher course.

Our basic advice is to learn to reflect back. When your child calls and says wistfully, "I really wish my roommate would talk to me more," as a parent you can open that conversation or shut it down. Responding with something such as, "You'd like for her to say more to you?" acknowledges that you heard her concern and want her to elaborate on the information that she initiated. This furthers the conversation and puts it back in your child's hands to extend her line of thinking. She might say something like, "Yeah, when I come in at night she's always reading, and that's when I want to talk," and the conversation can proceed from there as she begins to unravel the problem herself. Avoid saying "Yes, I had a roommate like that" or "Have you talked to the dean about switching?" or any of a set of suggestions about what to do, even something seemingly as helpful as "Have you tried being the one to get conversations going with her?" Don't leap to suggestions. Listen. Give her the space to talk aloud and figure out the problem and make it one she herself can solve.

---

**Practice This Role-Play**

Imagine that you're talking with a good friend and you say, "I'm having doubts about whether I want to stay with this job or make a career change." Now envision a possible set of responses your friend might offer:

A. "That's ridiculous! This is what you always said you wanted to do, and it's a secure field!"

B. "You should stick it out another year and then we'll talk."

C. "Sounds as though you're not sure this is the right thing for you."

Which response would you prefer to hear, and why? Where is each of these conversations likely to go? How would you feel in each case, and what would you be likely to say?

Now try the following:

Your son calls and says, "I don't think I want to be a math major anymore, and I'm really liking anthropology." Consider that you might offer any of the same responses. What is he likely to experience with each of these replies? What's the likely outcome?

---

## Use Noncontrolling Language

Language influences whether individuals feel that their autonomy is supported, whether in the home, in a classroom, or in the workplace. One simple word to try eliminating is "should" (and any variants, such as "must" and "have to"). Students who hear "You should be studying tonight and not going to that play rehearsal" or "You should choose a major that guarantees a good salary" are likely to retreat. This closes the conversation and shifts your role as a parent from trusting confidant to police sergeant.

When parents in one of Barbara's workshops practiced role-plays centered around common issues likely to arise during the first year of college, several reported that they were stunned to see how often the word "should" crept into their replies, even after having been forewarned. They also commented on how it felt when they were role-playing the student to be told they "should" do something (not so good!), and how active listening worked so much more effectively.

It isn't easy to train ourselves in this way, but it's well worth the practice, and the benefits are often immediately evident. Below are some other potential scenarios.

---

### More Role-Plays

Interest in changing majors is just one of the likely issues you might hear that will leave you wondering what to say in response. Try practicing your responses to a few others and generate some potential replies that might open conversations rather than close them off.

1. "My roommate and I just don't get along, and I don't know what to do."

---

2. "I'm feeling really stressed out. Midterms are next week, I've got three papers to write, we've got an out-of-town game, and I just don't see how I'll do everything that I have to do. And did I tell you I auditioned for an a cappella group? And we're going skiing this weekend!"

3. "I have the most interesting new friend! I've never known anyone from———who believed in———and it's really opening my eyes and I'm starting to wonder if I really believe———."

4. "I got a C on a calculus exam! I'm terrible at this! I want to drop the course!"

## Be Willing to Talk about Tough Topics

Development during the college years often involves a reexamination of beliefs and values, a process of establishing *value autonomy.* This process can create turmoil in some families, particularly if the exploration leads in directions that are at odds with parental beliefs and values. Some of the hardest phone calls might be when your child begins to talk about not going to church anymore, attending a political rally on a controversial topic, or sexual identity issues. As difficult as these calls might be, try to keep the door open and be accepting of your child and open-minded about hearing what she wants to tell you. When we asked students what they avoided talking to parents about, politics and religion were mentioned often. If these topics really are too difficult to discuss, perhaps students are making a wise choice in being silent.

## Promote Independent Decision Making

*Behavioral autonomy* involves capable, independent decision making—not necessarily without consultation, however. Help your children know what kind of decisions they can make themselves, and help them feel confident about doing so. College requires a vast set of decisions, small and large, academic and social: what courses to take, whether to get up for class or sleep in, what clubs to join, what parties to attend, whether and where to study abroad, what to major in. When you're consulted about any of the decisions that arise, do what you can to nurture good decision making rather than making the decision yourself. When your son begins to make some decisions without you, for example, choosing his own courses after consultation with an advisor, celebrate his growing independence. When your daughter says, "I can't decide whether to major in English or econ. What do you think?" try "Well, tell me more about what *you're* thinking" before offering an opinion.

## Know the College Resources and Promote Help-Seeking

Another valuable skill to be learned throughout adolescence and young adulthood is knowing when, how, and where to seek help. Learning to identify one's own needs and seeking the resources for assistance is a large part of growing up and becoming responsible for oneself. College campuses, even in a time of budget crises, provide a wide array of services to meet the academic and developmental needs of their students; these include the simple posting of office hours by a professor or teaching assistant, offering walk-in help. Yet it is surprising how little some students use this resource. Getting help from an instructor by asking questions about a topic that came up in class, clarifying an assignment, or discussing a possible paper topic is also a way for students to get to know the instructor and to have one who also knows them. Richard Light, a Harvard professor and author of *Making the Most of College*, suggests that each semester a student make it a goal to get to know at least one professor. This is wisdom worth passing on to your child, not as a mandate, but as a recommendation.

There are many other sources of support. When students are preparing papers, they need to know where to find what colleges refer to as "authorized assistance" and to learn to take advantage of these resources when needed. Sometimes this is made evident in a course syllabus, particularly if there are tutors or teaching assistants available for the course or department. Some institutions have a campus writing center, where writing tutors are available by appointment or during walk-in hours. If a child calls or emails you with a plea for proofreading or editing, suggest these alternatives.

College websites have an abundance of information, and your son or daughter can generally find assistance this way. Of course you can also be prepared, knowing those resources yourself. This is particularly useful when your child is reaching out to you for emotional support, perhaps not knowing how to negotiate a conflict with a roommate or deal with a friend who seems depressed. Refer your child to the residential life staff, as usually there is someone close in age who can serve as a starting point for such a conversation, or the Dean of Students Office, and of course the counseling services.

## Foster Internal Standards

Help your kids as early as possible to learn to develop internal standards and self-worth, not dependent on your approval. Learning to do work on their own breeds self-confidence and competence, and not having to report every grade to someone else also fosters ownership of the outcomes. Among the nearly one thousand students in our Middlebury-Michigan study 58 percent reported that their parents expected to know their grades, at least some of the time, and half of those students said it was frequently the case. If you're one of those parents who expects this, stop and consider why, and whether this is just a habit left over from earlier years. Most important, think about what you plan to do with that information, and what the implications might be.

In our study we found that 50 percent of the students were getting rewarded by their parents for grades. This is seldom a good idea at any age, given its ability to squelch internal motivation. It's a particularly bad idea in college, as students need to be responsible for their academic outcomes, take pride in their own work, and learn from their mistakes. It can also breed dishonesty, as students can learn to value the grade above how it was achieved.

When students tell you their grades (even if you don't expect it), consider how to respond. Imagine the student who calls to say "Mom! I got an A on the European history test!" One common response is something along the lines of "That's so good, honey. I knew you could do it. You're so smart and we're proud of you." The response acknowledges the trophy, but where does the conversation go from there? The effect is likely to foster a desire to do more to please the parents, rather than the desire to do well as a personal accomplishment, or even more important, to view that grade simply as informative feedback about the work invested and the knowledge gained. Ideally, if students want deeply to learn, their desires are driven from within and toward a goal of mastering the material.

By contrast, imagine the following response: "Wow, honey, how does that feel?" This response opens a line of conversation that might proceed, "Really great! I worked so hard on this one. I went to the review session last night and then got together with friends to study more, and I can see how much it helped me." Or try "An A! You must have really worked hard." According to psychologist Carol Dweck, the latter response will also be more likely to foster a student's motivation to further invest in building her intelligence, while "ability feedback" (such as "You're so smart") leads a student to protect that image and avoid intellectual risk taking.

## Foster Healthy Mutuality: Help Them See You as a Person

Remember that learning to see you as a person apart from your role as mom or dad is one of the psychological steps your child has to take in order to develop autonomy. Researchers have generally stated that this happens later than some other aspects of autonomy development, and our research shows that there is progress in this aspect of autonomy during the first semester of college. One positive aspect to all the conversation going on between parents and college kids is that it can advance such awareness. When parents mention something about work or ask for an opinion about a situation in their own lives, a sense of greater mutuality develops in the conversation than when the student is simply reporting from the front lines of college in a one-directional conversation. The child begins to realize that his parents have lives too, and this can foster his progression toward autonomy as well as toward an adult relationship with his parents. So parents not only can model healthy parent-to-child interactions but also can gradually introduce this type of adult-to-adult conversation.

## Know When It's Actually Worth Helping or Intervening, and When It's Not

Providing support for autonomy can sometimes conflict with a desire to be helpful or to be needed, even if your child is no longer at home.

245

Recognize that it's in your child's best interest to do many things for himself. Think carefully when your child asks you to do something that he can do alone, and instead help him figure out how to do it, if needed.

"YES, MOTHER, I TOLD YOU, I'M DOING FINE ON MY OWN AT COLLEGE.... HEY, COULD YOU LOG ON AND FIND MY SCHEDULE, ORDER MY BOOKS AND CALL ME WHEN IT'S TIME FOR CLASS?"

JIM BORGMAN ©2006 Cincinnati Enquirer. Reprinted with permission of UNIVERSAL UCLICK. All rights reserved.

Although sometimes your child will ask directly for help, recognize that in some cases she is just complaining because you're willing to listen. ("I got a C on this test and this professor is terrible! I don't know why he's even teaching at the college!") Don't translate these concerns into a need for action on your part.

We recommend that you not pick up your phone and call the college or university unless it is absolutely necessary. There are times when it's not worth getting overwrought, and when getting involved can decrease the college personnel's respect for the student. For instance, avoid calling coaches to increase playing time, calling professors about graded work, talking to dining services about college food, or trying to get a dean to engineer a roommate swap. If health and safety are involved, of course you should take action, for example, if your child's roommate is actually dangerous and not just disagreeable or a bad match, or if your child has medical issues around eating that need to be addressed. But first find out what your child has done on her own to handle the situation. Find out what else she thinks she could do. Parental intervention is a last resort. And don't start at the top. Presidents are very busy people, and they are often deluged with parental complaints about commonplace issues (e.g., quality of dining hall food) that detract from the important work they are doing. They also remember names.

Do not intervene in your child's workplace. Even though there is a lot of discussion about companies becoming more parent-friendly, it is generally just a bad idea. The company hired your child, not you, and your child needs to learn how to conduct himself effectively with coworkers and bosses. We suggest that you be sensitive about visiting. Some employers smirk about such behavior and are likely to see your child as less capable of operating independently.

## Keep Long-term Goals in Mind

As parents, we naturally want our children's lives to go well, and this sometimes keeps us, and our kids, overly focused on the moment. When a child calls for help with a paper it can be easy to want to be there for her and to help her achieve a good grade in that class. You might also be looking ahead, perhaps thinking that this particular paper will be important in the course grade, and the course grade is important on the transcript, and the transcript will be important when she applies to graduate school. That's understandable, but if you stop to think carefully about deeper long-term outcomes it's easier to see that it might not be in the best interest of your child to provide such support. This applies to calling a dean to get a roommate switch, or looking up courses for him for registration, or whatever request arose in the recent cell phone call. Wouldn't it be better if she actually became a better writer while she is in college?

The bottom line is to keep in mind what kind of person is developing in the process. What kind of adult do you want to help your child become? How do you want him to be viewed by employers? Prospective spouses? Friends and colleagues?

Learning to stay connected while letting go in the college years and beyond is another skill on the long road toward helping your child advance to adulthood. We encourage you to talk with fellow parents, your spouse, and your child about the ideas in this book. You may find that technology has altered your parenting practices in subtle ways that work at cross-purposes to your goals for your child's development. We also encourage you to discuss with others how to change what seems to be "the new normal" if it appears not to be in the best interests of healthy parenting. Parents can be as culpable as teens in thinking that, if everyone else is doing it, it must be okay; the current pattern of overcommunication is fed by this kind of thinking. Make a pact with friends to pull it back together, to perhaps talk less often and more deeply, and to permit your college-age children to allow other relationships to flourish as well—with new friends, professors, advisors, and other adults who are also invested in their development. Our research and reporting tell us that these years can be some of the best imaginable in your lives as parents. We hope you find this guidance useful.

# Notes

## Chapter 1

6    *built on research she had pursued several years earlier*: Hofer, B. K. & Yu, S. L. (2003). Teaching self-regulated learning through a "Learning to Learn" course. *Teaching of Psychology, 30*(1), 30–33.

9    *which psychologist Jeffrey Arnett calls "emerging adulthood"*: Arnett, J. J. (2000). Emerging adulthood: A theory of development from the late teens through the twenties. *American Psychologist, 55,* 469–480.

9    *The median age of first marriage has risen*: U.S. Bureau of the Census, www.census.gov.

## Chapter 2

19    *new survey of nearly a thousand students and their parents:* 918 students (64 percent female), average age 19.8, 97 percent between 18 and 22; 159 parents.

23    *students in the survey were a diverse group*: We used a random stratified sample for the Michigan participants; of the overall sample

from both schools, 81.7% were white, 14.1% Asian American, 3.4% African American, 8% Mexican American, 3.0% other Latino, 1.2% Native American, .4% Native Hawaiian, 3.1% other.

## Chapter 3

35    *Psychologists view autonomy as a basic human need*: Deci, E. L., & Ryan, R. M. (1987). The support of autonomy and the control of behavior. *Journal of Personality and Social Psychology, 53,* 1024–1037.

36    *It starts in early adolescence*: Steinberg, L., & Silverberg, S. (1986). The vicissitudes of autonomy in early adolescence. *Child Development, 57*(4), 841–851.

39    *"the blessing of a skinned knee,"*: Mogel, W. (2001). *The blessing of a skinned knee.* New York: Penguin Compass.

43    *fraught with conflict*: Measures of parental relationships were adapted from multiple sources, modified for a college population, and then supplemented with questions written by the research team, resulting in four scales: companionship (4 items, $\alpha$ = 0.80), mutuality (3 items, $\alpha$ = 0.73), conflict (5 items: $\alpha$ = 0.91), and control (3 items: $\alpha$ = 0.70).

46    *how students regulated their own academic work*: Questions were from the Motivated Strategies for Learning Questionnaire. See Pintrich, P. R., Smith, D. A. F., Garcia, T., & McKeachie, W. J. (1993). Reliability and predictive validity of the Motivated Strategies for Learning Questionnaire (MSLQ). *Educational and Psychological Measurement, 53,* 801–813.

46    *they were also far less likely to procrastinate:* Questions were from Wolters, C. (2003). Understanding procrastination from a self-regulated learning perspective. *Journal of Educational Psychology, 95,* 179–187.

46    *becoming a self-regulated learner:* Hofer, B., Yu, S., & Pintrich, P. (1998). Teaching college students to be self-regulated learners. In

D. Schunk & B. Zimmerman (Eds.), *Self-regulated learners: From teaching to self-reflective practice* (pp. 57–85). New York: Guilford.

## Chapter 9

184    *one in five college students in their study had a problem with alcohol:* Blanco, C., et al. (2008). Mental health of college students and their non–college-attending peers: Results from the National Epidemiologic Study on Alcohol and Related Conditions. *Archives of General Psychiatry, 65*(12):1429–1437.

199    *About 11 percent of college students met criteria for a mood disorder:* Ibid.

## Chapter 11

238    *"how to talk so your kids will listen and listen so your kids will talk":* For more information about active listening, see Adele Faber and Elaine Mazlish's books on this topic, including *How to talk so kids will listen & listen so kids will talk* (New York: Harper Paperbacks, 1999) and *How to talk so teens will listen & listen so teens will talk* (New York: William Morrow, 2005).

# Acknowledgments ----------------------------------------

### B.K.H.

I couldn't have done this research alone, nor would it have had the authenticity and vitality that a team of remarkable and dedicated undergraduates provided. They know these issues firsthand, and they were eager to dive into the literature, help create surveys, interpret data, and question, challenge, and continue to refine the work from one study to the next. I am particularly indebted to Elena Kennedy, who began as a summer research student when I thought this would be one small, finite project and who agreed to take it on as her honors thesis. She was masterful at every stop of the process, and it has been a pleasure to become collaborators and friends.

I am also especially appreciative of Christine Barratt, who helped me launch this project with the initial focus groups, and to Nancy Fullman and Catherine Timmins, who each took on significant portions of this research as their honors thesis work, advancing the research in new directions, with enthusiasm and caring attention to detail. Thanks also to the research dream team, Katie Hurd, Connie Souder, Lacee Patterson, John LoPresto, and Glenn Bickley, who took

Katie's pressing concerns about the positive side of the "tether" and helped develop measures to assess relationships with parents in the college years. ChakFu Lam, although involved in an entirely different research project with me, was generous in his assistance with teaching the complexities of complex survey software throughout this project.

My research on student-parent communication grew out of both my teaching and research interests, and I am blessed to be at a place where such things happen readily and are nurtured. My deep appreciation to all those at Middlebury College who have helped along the way, and especially to my colleagues in the Department of Psychology and students in my adolescent development course, who continue to teach me about the intricacies of emerging adulthood and inspire me to want to learn more.

Ann Hanson, former Dean of Student Affairs at Middlebury, has provided support as a friend and colleague at every step of the process, and she facilitated access to students for the initial surveys. Malinda Matney, Senior Research Associate for the Division of Student Affairs at the University of Michigan, was instrumental in making it possible for the research to be conducted there as well. I thank both Ann and Malinda also for providing opportunities to speak to student affairs staff at both institutions about the results.

This research would not have been possible without the cooperation of the students and parents who completed lengthy questionnaires, participated in focus groups, and shared their thoughts in interviews, and I am grateful for their time and their candor. Funding from the National Science Foundation program Research Experiences for Undergraduates helped launch this study, and it was expanded with assistance through the Paul P. Fidler Award from the National Center for the First Year Experience and Students in Transition. I am also grateful to those at the National Center, particularly Barbara Tobolowsky and Nina Glisson, for opportunities to speak about the results at two of their national conferences.

Social science researchers present their work mostly to each other, but it was in just such a setting at the American Psychological Association annual meeting where I first met agent Linda Loewenthal, probably the only nonpsychologist who attended my talk. I appreciate her vision, her initiative, her kind and generous manner, her cheerleading, her wisdom about writing and coauthoring, and her assistance to Abby and me every step of the way. My thanks also to Chris Wolters, who organized that APA session and invited me to participate. Thank you to colleagues at APA and at the Society for Research on Child Development meetings, where we presented this research, for their constructive feedback and ideas. I am forever grateful to Paul Pintrich, mentor extraordinaire, for infusing me with a love of research and the desire to communicate results to others who may find them of use.

I have colleagues at Middlebury who share the sense that scholarship can and should be brought to a wider audience, and a faculty reading/writing group that focused on this topic was another catalyst. Thank you to Peggy Nelson, Rebecca Gould, Laurie Essig, and Robert Schine for their support and encouragement and for leading by example.

I am indebted to public relations gurus at Middlebury, Sarah Ray and Blair Kloman, who helped bring the research to the media early on, in spite of my initial protests. Thank you to Bob Clagett, Dean of Admissions, who saw the value of this research to his admissions staff and invited me to present the work at their annual retreat. Thank you to Katie Smith Abbot for opportunities to present to parents and to David Bain for sage advice at the right moment.

I am ever appreciative of a wide community of friends for their listening, caring, and wise counsel— especially Rebecca Gould, Ann Hanson, Peggy Sax, Cynthia Packert, Nancy Belkov, Jeff Parker, Ava Slemrod, Gale Sinatra, and my dear grad school friends, Allison Ryan and Helen Patrick. Special thanks to my sister, Beverly McCay, for support always, and for providing me with writing space and time on the beach where we grew up.

Coauthoring a book has been an enormous learning experience, and I thank Abby for her patience, generosity, insights, journalistic savvy, good ideas, and continued faith in the project and in our ability to work together toward common goals. Thanks also to her husband J.D. for watching over us.

Thanks to our editor Leslie Meredith and associate editor Donna Loffredo for their interest in the story Abby and I wanted to tell together and for all their help in bringing that story to the printed page.

Most important, utmost thanks to my adult children, Selene and Zach, who have taught me so much about parenting and how to stay connected while letting go. I continue to learn from them both and I'm grateful for their love and support.

**A.S.M.**

Many people have helped me in the reporting and writing of the book, but no one more than my beloved husband, John D. Moore, who is himself a superb editor and writer, coach and partner, and matchless attorney. My children, Jack and Carlos, also have been a wellspring of support—*"Come on Mom, you can do it!"* I also want to give thanks to my sister, Lynn Moran, who spent countless hours reading copy, giving smart advice, and cheering me along the way.

I am ever grateful to my friends for all the different ways that they helped me: Jacque Metheney for her perpetually sympathetic ear, commonsense approach, and willingness to always help in a pinch (in writing this book, there were many); Anne and Tom Condon, two extraordinary writers and editors, for their constant personal and professional support; Jocelyn McClurg, one of the best writers whom I have read and know, for her unwavering interest, humor, and willingness to listen; Diane McAndrews for her unshakeable confidence in me and the meals that she made for my family during the book's busiest times; Susan Panisch, attorney and Northwestern colleague, for her tireless counsel and friendship; Susan Noyes Bennetto for her constant enthusiasm and encouragement; Marie Flaherty and Veronica Badiola for supporting my work and understanding all the get-togethers and birthdays missed because of deadlines; and Ted Strayer, D.O., who has kept me going, both body and soul.

I also want to thank all the students and parents whom I met while reporting this book. Their candor and insight have enriched my life and this book. My list, of course, would not be complete without noting all the college professors, deans, and administrators who shared their stories and wisdom. The same goes for the teachers and counselors in the elementary, middle, and high school years—all provided valuable insights. Thanks also to the professionals in the mental health and learning disability communities who patiently helped shape our chapters on these key subjects. Writing with a coauthor, and one in a career so different from mine, has been an adventure! Thank you, Barbara, for sharing your world and expertise on both a personal and professional level with me. We have come a long way from our first August meeting in a Brattleboro coffee shop to write this book together, and in the process have learned so much.

Our agent, Linda Loewenthal at the David Black Literary Agency, a smart editor, unflappable advocate, and good friend, also has won my heartfelt appreciation and admiration.

Finally, a note of gratitude to Free Press editors Leslie Meredith and Donna Loffredo for their expert editing, patience, and empathy.

# Index

# About the Authors ----------------------------------------------

Barbara K. Hofer, Ph.D., is a professor of psychology at Middlebury College who studies educational and developmental issues in adolescence and the transition to adulthood. Dr. Hofer earned an Ed.M. in Human Development from Harvard University and a Ph.D. in Education and Psychology from the University of Michigan. The author of many chapters and articles in psychological and educational journals and books, she is a Fellow of the American Psychological Association and the recipient of national awards for teaching, research, and writing from APA and the American Educational Research Association. The parent of a daughter and a son who recently completed college, she knows the issues of parenting this generation firsthand.

Abigail Sullivan Moore has been a regular contributor to the *New York Times,* writing about college and university issues and other topics. Early in her career Abby also worked as a staff writer for the *Hartford Courant.* She has extensive experience in the corporate sector, having taken a midcareer break from journalism to work at Travelers in media relations and later to serve as a director of corporate relations at CIGNA Corporation. She also has been a stay-at-home mom and is the parent of two adolescent boys, whom she hopes to raise into caring and competent young adults. She holds a B.A. from the University of Pennsylvania and an M.S. in Journalism from the Medill School of Journalism at Northwestern University.